MORE THAN MEETS THE EYE

This book is dedicated to
HUGH L. KEENLEYSIDE
in gratitude for his
innumerable acts of kindness,
in admiration, and in
lively affection.

MORE THAN MEETS THE EYE
The Life and Lore of Western Wildflowers

Watercolor paintings & text
by J. WARD-HARRIS

with a foreword by J. Fenwick Lansdowne

Toronto
OXFORD UNIVERSITY PRESS
1983

Produced by Roger Boulton
Designed by Fortunato Aglialoro (Studio 2 Graphics)

Canadian Cataloguing in Publication Data

Ward-Harris, Joan.
More than meets the eye

Includes index.
ISBN 0-19-540437-8

1. Wild flowers—Canada, Western—Identification.*
I. Lansdowne, J. F. (James Fenwick), 1937–
II. Title.

QK203.W37W47   582.13′09712   C83-098237-X

© Oxford University Press (Canadian Branch) 1983
Oxford is a trademark of Oxford University Press

ISBN 0-19-540437-8

1 2 3 4 - 6 5 4 3

Printed in Hong Kong by
Everbest Printing Company Limited

Foreword

The natural world is a source of happiness and comfort to many people. In becoming absorbed by some aspect of it they find the peace of mind that daily life so frequently denies. There are so many things there to engage us and hold our interest, but surely nothing is so immediately attractive or gives such spontaneous pleasure as the wildflowers.

Wildflowers brighten all seasons; in spring and summer the countryside is bedecked with blossoms while later the air of autumn is full of blowing seeds and the winter hedgerows are decorated with vivid fruits and berries. The casual eye unconsciously notes them and the heart lifts, for wildflowers have the perennial power to cheer us, whether we be country-living people or city dwellers.

Few places are so barren that no flowers will grow. Some bloom secretively in the damp shade of woods or can be found entangled in the rank field growth of high summer. Others cling to precipitous sides of canyons or spring up bravely in the wake of retreating snows to carpet alpine meadows.

Many, however, flourish in more prosaic and inhospitable situations, where they may bring pleasure to those who have little chance to escape the urban landscape. Between the ties of railway tracks and on their embankments little associations of wild plants thrive, and vacant lots, when explored, may prove to be wild gardens. Here the inhabitants go through their seasonal cycles unnoticed and undisturbed. These opportunist plants accommodate themselves wherever their seeds lodge—in a broken wall or a pavement crack. Who has not seen such a flower in indomitable bloom? Perhaps it was only a dandelion with its tattered, brilliant sunbursts or a spire of pink fireweed, dwarfed to a height of inches by the poverty of its home, but these, common and despised plants that they are, have all the intrinsic beauty of rarer species as well as a resilience quite in contrast to their apparent fragility.

With this new book, artist and writer Joan Ward-Harris has produced a comprehensive and practical handbook picturing and describing some of the wildflowers of the four western provinces of Canada and of the American states adjoining them. It is a guide that will be a useful and instructive companion to the less knowledgeable amateur and a reliable reference book for serious students. Her sensitive and beautiful illustrations show Mrs Ward-Harris to be a botanical artist in the best tradition, one who has depicted her subjects with skill and evident love. Rendered in the watercolor that is such an appropriate medium for the painting of flowers, the illustrations show all species described in the text.

The plant descriptions and the text in general match the paintings in clarity and interest. To the person just newly come to the study of wildflowers, the writer's wise and lively information on the enjoyment and protection of plants will be welcome and valuable, while her emphasis on the use of correct names and on the understanding of them should please the professional botanist.

The pleasure of identifying wildflowers with the aid of Joan Ward-Harris's book will be considerably increased by her explanation of names, both common and scientific. There is a charm in these: even the Latin of the scientists, so forbidding at first encounter, is usually descriptive and sometimes whimsical, while the everyday names of wildflowers are perhaps the most allusive and delightful in the whole lexicon of natural history. So they seem to be in all languages, for the perfection of flowers stimulates the human mind to a correspondingly delicate fancy. These names alone might form the material for hours of pleasurable contemplation, to take our thoughts far beyond the confines of botany and down avenues of literature and folklore and mythology.

In exquisitely detailed paintings and with encyclopedic knowledge, Joan Ward-Harris reveals her instinctive sympathy for and understanding of the plants and flowers of her western home. We are fortunate that in her writing she is able to impart something of them to us and to kindle in us the beginning of a similar love.

Victoria, B.C.,　　　　　　　J. FENWICK LANSDOWNE
January 1983　　　　　　　　O.C., R.C.A.

Acknowledgments

In offering thanks for help rendered, first and foremost I must single out Dr R.T. Ogilvie, British Columbia's Curator of Botany, who interrupted his busy schedule many times to make helpful suggestions relating to this book. He also loaned me valuable reference works from his private collection, and then nobly read the finished manuscript.

I wish also to acknowledge assistance given in the early phases of planning the book by botanists Dr J. Maze (who read the first draft) and Dr Roy Taylor, and ethnobotanist Dr Nancy J. Turner.

Being both an artist and a lifelong student of botany I launched myself into this project with confidence. It was not until I decided to incorporate into the text something more than purely botanical information and therefore ventured into somewhat esoteric research, that I began canvassing other experts for confirmation of my findings before etching them in stone.

I am indebted to Sir Robin Mackworth-Young, K.C.V.O., Chief Librarian to Her Majesty the Queen, for his prompt, detailed, and authoritative confirmation of royalty's historical use of the fleur-de-lis as an heraldic device. In this connection I also thank that ebullient historian, Professor Sydney W. (Toby) Jackman, whose total recall on almost any subject has staggered me for years.

I elicited snippets of information from all manner of people, ranging from entomologists to ecclesiastics, medicos to medievalists, weavers to woodsmen. I am particularly grateful to Dr Richard A. Ring, who increased my 'beetlemania' with some lively life histories, and to Patricia Crofton, who revealed the fascinations of weaving and plant dyes.

And what would we do without the help of our modest, always eager-to-please librarians? I have reason to be grateful to Molly MacGregor-Greer, Alice Solyma, and Don White, as well as to the cheerful and painstaking staff in the reference department of the Greater Victoria Public Library.

Naturally none of those mentioned above can be blamed for any errors or omissions in the text; responsibility for the finished product is mine alone.

The paintings in this book have been done from living wild specimens, but I have needed to study some of them over a longer period than that afforded me in the field. Ernest Lythgoe, A. Smith, and Rebecca Wyngert—wildflower gardeners of the first rank—helped to bridge the gap and I owe them an ongoing debt of gratitude for the loan of specially potted show quality plants and for gifts of rare specimens for my own garden.

Special thanks are due to Roger Boulton, formerly of Oxford University Press, who not only graciously accepted suggestions in areas where authors are not supposed to meddle, but also took endless pains and exercised great ingenuity to accommodate the whole of my text, where lesser editors would simply have cut it. For such sensitive treatment I am truly grateful.

Lastly, it is my pleasure once again to record thanks to my husband, Edward Ward-Harris, for taking time from his own work of literary criticism and lecturing, for endless discussions and editorial comment relating to my work. No one else has the temerity to criticize my efforts so forcefully—but with such a salutary effect. His tact and humor ensured that two writers living under the same roof remained on speaking terms—no mean feat!

Contents

Introduction

I will be the gladdest thing under the sun!
I will touch a hundred flowers and not pick one.
Edna St Vincent Millay: Afternoon on a Hill (1917)

Western Canada is an awful lot of geography. The four provinces—British Columbia, Alberta, Saskatchewan, and Manitoba—cover more than one million square miles or 2.5 million square kilometers, and that is more than one-third of the total area of the United States, or eleven times the size of the United Kingdom, or almost as large as India. British Columbia alone is so immense that France, West Germany, Belgium, and the Netherlands could be fitted into it and still leave room for the whole of Kenya!

When you look at land in that way and take into account the variables of terrain and climate, you begin to appreciate that the range of plant habitats is impressively varied. And when you visualize in your mind's eye the contrasts—the vast plains and prairies; the unexpected Cypress Hills bordering southern Alberta and Saskatchewan; the Riding Mountain Range in southern Manitoba, which forms an oasis of boreal forest in the endless prairie; the foothills of western Alberta rising to the magnificent Rocky Mountains, beyond which lie the grasslands, semi-desert, forests, and beaches of British Columbia—and when you go on to realize that each region and sub-region has its share of wildflowers, often in breathtaking abundance, then the wonder of it all becomes apparent.

Not all species of wildflowers are dealt with in the following pages—there are roughly 2,000 species in British Columbia alone, for heaven's sake! But you will find illustrated in this book a selection of the most widely spread wildflowers, as well as some that are too beautiful or exceptionally interesting to be left out.

Every flower illustrated is to be found in British Columbia. This is simply because the diversity of climatic zones makes B.C. especially hospitable to a rich variety of plant life. But most of the plants shown are common to the four western provinces. In fact some are so wide-spread that they are circumboreal. And because nature takes no account of artificial, man-made boundaries, the same plants are of course to be found in adjacent areas of the United States, particularly in Washington and Oregon, where *all* the flowers illustrated are to be seen.

I have written the text and painted the flowers for this book to stimulate the interest of general readers who want to learn more about the wildflowers they come across, in particular their correct names. To achieve this you must become familiar with a modicum of Latin which, contrary to popular belief, is useful for more things than just 'the judging'. In fact, without Latin (the use of which dates back to the time when it was the international academic form of communication) there would be botanical chaos.

Common names are sometimes inaccurate. For instance, prairie crocus is not a crocus and the name 'lady's-slipper' applies to several different flowers. Also, when plants are introduced to another locality or country they acquire new common names, thus adding to the confusion. Botanists have solved the problem by giving each plant a Latin name that is understood everywhere. Try it—it's not difficult. If you can (and you do) pronounce words like 'victorious', 'campanula', 'digit', and scores of other words that are either Latin words or derivations from Latin, then you will have no problem reading botanical names.

Apart from identification, Latin serves another purpose: it frequently permits you to locate a specific plant. For example, *palustris* means 'of the swamp', and *arvense* means 'a field', so you know at once where to look.

There are lots of things you should know about plants in general and about this book in particular, and these things deserve separate mention.

Why Bother About Plants?

Man likes to think of himself as the ultimate in evolution and to consider that every other living thing on earth was put there expressly for his purpose, to be exploited and squandered at will. The facts belie this belief, but most people ignore them and let the comforting illusion persist. We do so at our peril, of course, and the warning should be screamed from the housetops; but as every politician knows, battles are not won by telling unpalatable truths.

It is not my intention to add yet another tract in support of the conservation lobby; this is not that kind of book. But at the same time, to ignore the subject completely would be unforgivable. So, as a compromise, I'll leave the main argument in the capable hands of others and confine myself to the plant world.

It is true that despite pollution and reckless over-exploitation the oceans continue to produce annual, albeit diminishing, harvests of food; but one can state categorically that on land, without green plants life as we know it would cease, for all food for man and beast comes from them. Moreover, they manufacture the very oxygen we breathe (while making good use of the carbon dioxide we exhale), so without green plants (don't forget that trees are also plants) we would suffocate. We would also starve, but having suffocated that would be academic.

Plants live on solar power. Energy from sunlight is trapped by chlorophyll in their green leaves which, with water and nutrients from the soil and carbon dioxide from the air, are used to build simple sugars to nourish the plants. The process is called photosynthesis (Greek *photos*—light; and Latin *synthesis*—a putting together). The process ceases at night, when the reverse takes place (respiration, whereby food is chemically broken down). Ingenious man, with all the resources of science at his disposal, will never be able to devise a way to produce adequate food material with sustaining body-building nourishment to come anywhere near the perfection achieved by the plant cell, perfection all of us take for granted.

Because neither human nor animal is able to produce food by photosynthesis, both man and beast must rely on plants for their very existence. In our case we have to eat either the plants themselves or the animals that feed on them. The preservation of plants, therefore, is a straightforward matter of self-interest and that, in a nutshell, is the case for conservation.

The thing to remember is that a plant's green leaves give it sustenance and, directly or indirectly, provide food for us. Green leaves, therefore, should always be left growing. But, you may ask, if leaves are that important, how do plants whose leaves have been eaten by animals manage to survive? The answer is that the wholesale death of plants can occur in any area where domesticated animals are confined in overcrowded conditions, or when wild animals, such as elephants, are confined in too great numbers to a restricted wildlife park area. But in the real wild, providing that there is a proper balance between the number of herbivorous animals and their particular food ranges, plantlife is rarely destroyed.

The proviso is important. Ground-feeding herbivores such as rabbits, or a herd of deer browsing on the move, will overgraze if they are too numerous for their given areas. Plant destruction and eventual starvation will result. But if plants and animals, including, of course, natural animal predators, are left alone, nature always achieves a correct balance. It is really very simple. Nature is tolerant, but when man, the greatest predator and interferer of all, goes too far, she retaliates. Wouldn't you?

Ironically, contributing to the extinction of some wildflowers is their very beauty. By ripping and tearing to secure a stem bearing a gorgeous bloom, particularly a lily, leaves are lost, for the stem is taken too near the ground. Not only is the flower prevented from producing seed but the violent act will also have disturbed the bulb, and with no leaves bringing it nourishment from above, a lily will die, or at least take years to recover from the shock.

Mention of bulbs brings me to the often ignored subject of roots. Out of sight, out of mind. Roots of some plants benefit man by fixing nitrogen from the air in nodules in the roots through bacterial action. In nitrogen-deficient soil (such as bogs, swamps, or depleted domestic fields or gardens) these root nodules release their nitrogen and so assist plants to a complete 'diet' that would otherwise have been leached out by rain, melting snow, or other depletors.

Roots help to bind soil and prevent erosion, which carried to extreme produces dustbowls and deserts. And tree roots (admittedly somewhat outside the compass of this book, although as I keep repeating, trees are plants) in addition to their anchorage role also help break down large rocks as they grope for nourishment and footholds. This is a fascinating phenomenon. First a crack appears on the rock's surface, then another, and in due course water seeps down the crevices and freezes in winter. The ice heaves the underlying structures, causing pieces of rock to move downward to rivers and eventually to the sea. On the long, slow journey, particles decrease in size until infinitesimal bits form pockets of soil in which small plants germinate, put down roots—and hold the soil together. Marvellous, isn't it?

Why bother about plants? Well, as you've seen, the short answer is that our very lives depend upon them. You could help, starting at the wildflower level, by looking and not picking. It's only a short step from there to agitating against wholesale, indiscriminate logging. If enough people become involved, and if it's not already too late, then—you never know—we might even ensure the survival of our species.

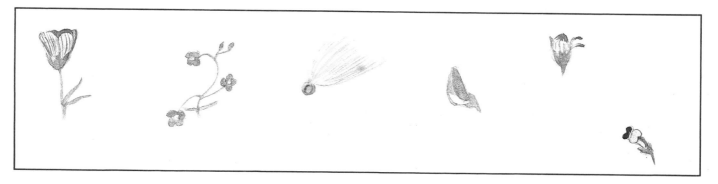

Looking at Plants

Family life in the Victorian age was, by all accounts, dreadfully dull for the ordinary person. Victorian boredom was made up of many things, but perhaps most disliked was the daily walk, known as 'a constitutional', or the practice of 'pedestrianism', words that aptly convey the tedium. This ennui persisted until mid-century, when a sudden craze for natural history enabled people to combine the compulsory walk with the study of botany, resulting in thousands of useless collections of pressed flowers. Anything to alleviate boredom!

We've come a long way since then. Today, thanks to pleas for conservation, most people are content to look at flowers without picking them. This can be a most rewarding hobby if you know how to look and what you are looking for.

All you require is a small pocket lens (x10) and a notebook in which to record the date of your find, its location, soil conditions, vegetation, and the plant's name (botanical, for sure; common name or names if you wish). Such notes stimulate interest, aid observation habits and memory, and may some day prove useful.

Where to look. Apart from the obvious places, you should make a habit of looking on vacant lots; remarkable things can happen on such sites. When the rubble was cleared from post-war London, wild plants not seen for hundreds of years began to appear. Their seeds had lain dormant for centuries beneath the crushing weight of buildings. In Egypt, where the clear dry climate is conducive to preservation, a bouquet of flowers, dead for 3,000 years, was found at the entrance to the tomb of King Tutankhamen. Modern science determined not only what the wildflowers were but when they bloomed, placing the date of the pharaoh's burial in late April or early May.

You are unlikely to discover anything quite so dramatic in your wanderings, but you will be pleasantly surprised by what you will find in a systematic search of roadside hedgerows, swampy areas, the shores of lakes and the sea, and in gravel pits (unlikely but useful sources of plantlife).

If you live in year-round wildflower country, try marking a few favorites with durable plant labels so that you can check the increase or decrease of the crop the following year. If there is no trace of the plants when you return, mark the spot, as the flowers may yet reappear, a recurring phenomenon (see Indian pipe, page 38).

Looking for Details. First, take in the whole plant: the way the flower sits on its stem, how the leaves grow—in pairs or whorls, on opposite sides of the stem or alternately up it. Notice flower-buds: do they open from the bottom or from the top? How many stamens can you see? (Take one bloom and open it: you may be surprised at stamen placement.) When you find a flower with a number of 'petals' of the same color, can you distinguish petals from sepals? (Sepals grow outside petals.) It won't take long to discover that there are groups of plants with similar characteristics, such as the five petals of potentilla and the wild strawberry (rose family). Keen observation brings excitement in finding such oddities as a six-petalled wild strawberry flower.

Then there are the leaves: yellow-greens, gray-greens, blue-greens; even some that are white or gray, usually on the undersides. Some carry flower-color in their veins or on their edges; some are hairy, not to say slightly poisonous (stinging nettle); others are smooth and shiny, thick and leathery, or wafer-thin. All these characteristics have important functions for the well-being of the plant.

Stalks are interesting, too: look for round ones, or angled, square, flat, and sticky ones. Again, are they smooth or prickly? Solid or hollow? Some, such as the marsh-marigold (page 4) have brightly colored stems from the flower or leaf to ground level or below.

To a wildflower watcher, the beauty of a plant as a whole is satisfying, but observing details will increase the pleasure tenfold.

Your notes will be valuable, but it is a truism that you don't know an object until you have drawn it. So, if you can draw at all, do; the more you draw the more skilled you will become. Take photographs by all means, but a camera does not 'see' form or dimension and so is always second best.

To Pick or Not to Pick

As I said earlier, I am not going to preach about conservation. You know all the arguments already and it would be idle to recapitulate them here. In the next few pages I shall touch on transplanting wildflowers, but before doing so I feel I should make my own position clear. I only wish I could do so as succinctly as Edna St Vincent Millay, who wrote the lines quoted at the beginning of the introduction.

As a wildlife artist specializing in the painting of plants I am fanatical about the conservation of wildflowers (and all wildlife, for that matter) and I have done my share of proselytizing. I simply point out that the indiscriminate picking of wild plants adds to the number of endangered species, and that we have no right to deprive others, to say nothing of future generations, of the beauty that has so delighted us.

I find that most people are willing to listen to a reasoned, logical argument on this point, particularly when it is backed up by facts. Unfortunately, there will always be people who are not content until they possess the flowers they see growing wild, and when I encounter them the best I can do is to defend the plants by showing how they can be taken with the least amount of damage to the plant and its environment. If you see a large group of flowers, I tell them, and cannot resist the longing, *cut* a single specimen with a sharp knife, making sure you leave plenty of stem *and leaves*. I explain that the green leaves are the plant's food factory and that without them it will die or, in the case of bulbs, be drastically set back, perhaps for years.

Now interested, people usually ask questions and this permits me to point out not only the obvious—that picking prevents a flower from producing seed—but also the not so obvious things, such as how the yanking or breaking of a stem rocks the roots and harms the plant. I find that most people are eager to learn, and having learned, learn respect. When I told one group that the mass of flowers they were looking at was in fact the *only* large stand of specimens of that particular species left anywhere, and added for good measure that there would be a lot more if others hadn't said, 'Oh well, taking one won't hurt,' they were suitably chastened and, to my delight, instantly appointed themselves guardians of the area.

Education is the answer to thoughtless desecration. If a brief lesson given to a wandering group of strangers in a forest glade could produce more converts than a missionary can make in a month of Sundays, then just think what could be achieved by widespread informed instruction, beginning with children in the home and at school. Here I must include a word of praise for our parks naturalists, who perform an excellent service educating people on wild trails where marvellous plants thrive—provided they are not trodden upon or picked.

In the old days, when there seemed to be an endless supply of plants, ruthless harvesting methods were employed to collect plants for food and medicine, with devastating results. Today people know better and methods are used to ensure crop continuity.

Transplanting. I have seen otherwise responsible men and women—keen gardeners all—steal bits of plants from many a famous park or garden and furtively slip them into folded umbrellas or pockets. They belong to the legion of thieving transplanters whose repeated failures serve only to strengthen their resolve to succeed, which in most cases is precluded by abysmal ignorance.

Some wildflower books state that this or that plant can be moved 'easily'. Don't believe it! It takes skill, knowledge, and a lot of loving care to transfer wild plants to a domestic garden successfully. Conditions of soil and moisture must be right but rarely are. The plants must be transplantable—some species will not survive. The time of year should be right, too; it is hopeless to try to transplant in summer heat or icy cold. The result too often is disappointment and another dead plant flung on the compost heap.

Although I do not subscribe to the wholesale collecting of wildflowers, I do understand the fascination of having a wild garden of your own: indeed I have one, although it is very small.

First one must observe the fundamental rules. Know which plants can or cannot be moved. Obtain permission *without fail* from the private owner of property, the municipal authority where indicated, or even a building contractor. To collect as a trespasser is unforgivable. Be sure you are not about to take an endangered species. Have your home site prepared in advance. Take note of local weather and if possible wait until the right moment: spring-blooming flowers transplant best in the fall; summer bloomers in the following spring. Or one can wait for a month after blooms have faded, but the plants are less likely to survive.

Equipment should include plastic bags and twist ties; damp paper towels to wrap roots and cut stems; picnic cooler and ice to preserve specimens in bags; hand-trowel and small hand-fork; small hand-rake to tidy up after lifting (remember to replace ground litter); long-bladed, square-edged spade for deep-growing specimens; sharp pocket-knife or secateurs to cut alien roots entangled in your plant's roots; razor blades for cuttings, which should not be squeezed in secateurs. A useful though not absolutely necessary refinement is a soil-testing kit to help you duplicate the soil.

There are various ways of taking wild plants. Propagating from seed is the best because no damage is done to anything. Cuttings are next best.

To obtain seeds before birds, insects, or wind reach them first, tie a muslin bag over an unopened seed pod with a twist tie. Return when the seed is mature (watch the other pods and compare), cut the stem—and you have your seeds in the bag. Leave the other seed pods to nature.

Sow your seeds thinly in flats in a mixture of finely sifted compost or peat moss and sharp builder's sand in equal proportions, moistened (not soaked). Sift about a quarter of an inch of fine dry soil on top of the seeds (very tiny ones merely need to be scattered and gently pressed down). Protect from sun and rain, and when the seedlings have their first true leaves transplant them into individual pots until they grow sturdy enough to bed out. Composition pots are more expensive than clay, but since you plant the pot you don't disturb the seedling's roots and the pot merely rots away. Seeds that have to be kept should be dried away from sun, then bottled and stored in the refrigerator. Some seeds derive benefit from this treatment; some can even be frozen into ice cubes!

To obtain cuttings, razor-cut a small portion of root-bearing stem about four inches or ten centimeters long, from firm new growth having four or five leaves. Fine root hairs must not dry out, so rush your cuttings home in protective bags with some of their own soil and replant immediately. Water and protect from sun and wind until established. Rootless stem cuttings can be placed several to a pot of the seedling mixture and protected until roots have formed.

To obtain deep-growing subjects by digging, use the spade to dig several inches away from the dormant bulb or plant (mark the site while it is in bloom). If the soil is dry, water thoroughly before beginning the operation. These plants will assuredly die if you try to move them with green top-growth. Always replant quickly, before nightfall, and always mix some of the plant's own soil in the hole.

Because this is not a gardening book, I suggest that for further information you seek some of the excellent wildflower gardening books now available.

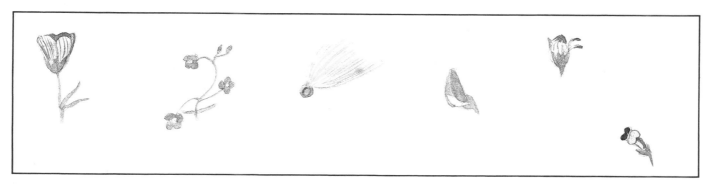

Things You Should Know

The majority of the flowers illustrated are common to the four western provinces and their counterparts in the U.S.A. Some are common to the whole continent. But there may be variations from one location to another and this has been noted as 'very close species' or 'close species' to avoid words such as 'form' and 'variety', which have different and distinct meanings in botany.

Very close species means any plant so similar to the one illustrated that only a botanist could tell the difference.

Close species means a plant that differs from the one illustrated but is easily recognizable by a layman.

Botanical names are provided for those who wish to study the minor differences further, and a list of references will be found at the end of the book.

Technical books on botany are arranged in order of families, and not always in the same order, which is confusing. This book is arranged by color, but as an artist I know that colors are not always what they seem. Some mauves are almost blue and some pinks are so close to mauve that arbitrary classification is tricky. Common names add to the confusion. For example, Blue Clematis is mauve. So, if a flower you think is red is not in the red section, try orange, some shades of which contain more red than yellow. Get the idea?

One further point while we are on the subject of color. Just as petunias or zinnias grow in your garden in a multitude of colors, so in wildflowers there can be a range of color in a species or genus to the extent that two flowers growing within inches of one another may be of separate colors but of the same species. It's somewhat perplexing, but you will just have to put up with it. I have tried to simplify, but botany is a complicated subject.

What Is a Plant?

All manner of growing things come under the heading of 'plants'. Mosses, lichens, and ferns are plants, as is the parsley in your garden. Did you realize that trees are also plants? (I've said this before.) And what about mushrooms? Well, scientists continue to argue about their classifications. To avoid hair-splitting, this book uses the word 'plant' to describe the unit of root, leaves, stem, and flower, whether growth takes place in the ground, on trees, or in the water.

If, like Ferdinand the Bull, you just want to smell the flowers, then stop right here. But if you are interested in

XIV

learning about elementary plant classification, then read on.

At first glance, classification and naming seems a haphazard affair. It isn't. Everything conforms to an international botanical code revised every five years by taxonomists—botanists whose word is the final authority. This ensures that botanists the world over can communicate with one another in a common language, Latin.

Plant Differences

If a flower you are trying to identify does not *exactly* match its portrait in this book, don't immediately assume it is a different species. The plant painted may have been growing miles from where you saw your specimen and its growth may have been influenced by the richness or other features of the soil and the amount of sunlight and moisture it received. Any or a combination of these conditions can affect a plant's size, color, and number of flowers. It is also conceivable that the plant painted may have reached a stage in its growth different from the one you saw. A casual glance is not good enough, but a brief comparative study, particularly of vital statistics, will usually establish identity.

Blooming Season

Because the flowers in this book come from such widely divergent areas, general flowering periods are given, cov-

ering locations from sea level to high mountains. For obvious reasons flowers bloom earlier on the west coast than in the prairie regions, where spring arrives later, and mountain flowers bloom after their counterparts at sea or plains levels have set seed. When summer advances and the prairies dry out, flowers whose season is over on the prairies are blooming in the cooler regions of the west. Wildflower-lovers, driving from the prairies to the coast, will find that these climatic changes add an extra dimension of pleasure to a holiday trip.

Plant Size

Height of plants is given at the beginning of each description and you will see that some plants vary in height considerably. This is because allowance has to be made for different conditions that determine probable minimum and maximum size. Rich soil will as a rule produce taller plants than poor, and in shady habitats some plants must stretch to obtain life-giving sunlight, to such an extent that they seem 'leggy' and pale, in contrast to those growing in full light that are often more compact. Rough mountain climates make for low-growing plants with moisture conserving leaves and more brilliant colors. Arid conditions also produce plants with moisture holding structures. Uniformity of size, as in stamped-out cookies, doesn't exist in the plant world.

Why Plants Have Seasons

All living things have an internal device which, for want of a better description, is known as a biological clock.

With one notable exception, all animals and plants obey the dictates of their respective clocks. Only man—who else?—interferes with the natural rhythm at will, jet-lag being the result of the best-known example.

The most dramatic manifestation of the biological or molecular clock at work is when migrating animals are 'informed' of the precise moment when they should take off. Less dramatic, but equally marvellous, is the dependence of insects on their clock to prompt them to sally forth by day or night in search of those flowers which,

regulated in turn by their own clocks, produce the nectar to attract and feed their pollinators.

Despite decades of work carried out all over the world, the location of the biological clock in plants has still to be established, although it is believed to be contained in the cell nucleus. Wherever it is, its smooth functioning and unfailing accuracy are vital to the survival of the species. It ordains not only the time of year at which a flower will bloom, but also the exact time of day, so that 'opening time' coincides precisely with the arrival of pollinating insects.

What happens then is a sexual exercise, but all parties

concerned are oblivious to the fact. Each flower produces its share of nectar but in such a way that attracted visitors have to work hard to get at some of it. They do this by probing with their probosces (butterflies have long ones and 'work' flowers with deep nectaries, as do humming-birds; bees have short ones, and so on). While an unsuspecting insect is busy feeding, the flower sheds pollen from its anthers (located at the tip of the stamen's filament, yellow pollen or male sperm being clearly visible) onto the creature's head, back, or legs. This is then carried to another nectar-laden flower of the same species and neatly transferred to the receptive female stigma by contact. And *voilà*, the deed is done, with little or no waste of precious pollen grains.

Different species of flowers release their nectar during specific hours at different times of day, so that insects ensure pollination of a particular species without waste of energy. One of nature's stringent rules is that no plant shall fertilize itself (unless it also has an alternative means of reproduction). There are many intricate methods employed: orchids are highly specialized and are worth special study. Skunk cabbage *(Lysichitum americanum)* is another example. It is pollinated *only* by colonies of one little brown beetle *(Pelecomalium testseeum*—it has no common name), which lives within the pale yellow spathe of this curious plant with the sickly smell. The spadix—a green column on which minute flowers grow in tight spirals—is covered with pollen, which the little beast carries from flower to flower until its job is done. The spathe withers, the spadix swells and grows tall, setting seed. Meanwhile the little beetle moves on to continue its life-cycle of egg-laying and pupation in the ground. It and the skunk cabbage have evolved complete synchronization.

The well-known cultivated *nicotiana* (tobacco plant) blooms at night. Its white flower buds, formed during the day, open and give off perfume only in the evening to attract night-flying moths to the nectar in their deep corollas. The flowers are wide, flattened, and tilted slightly upwards to facilitate entry. Neither butterfly nor hummingbird, in spite of their long nectar-gathering tongues, is interested, because no nectar is present in the scentless blossoms during daylight hours. If you watch this on a summer's evening you may also observe another phenomenon: a feeding moth may suddenly veer away from the flower at which it is hovering. There will probably be a small bat in the vicinity that has located the moth, which was warned just in time to move away from the flower's white surface.

To cite another daytime plant, I would like to describe the lovely chicory's behavior. It produces its nectar between the hours of seven a.m. and noon, and its principal pollinators are bees, whose 'blue vision' is excellent and who possess a phenomenal sense of time: they visit blue chicory flowers only during those five hours. Chicory puts on its gay display of many flowers, yet each lives but a day—long enough to be fertilized—then dies and is succeeded by the next higher on the stem. Bees do not, indeed cannot, waste time and effort visiting nectar-less blooms. Furthermore, plant and insect are synchronized for their mutual profit by a sort of disappearing act: when chicory flowers are closed there is no flag of recognition; the rather drab plant becomes so camouflaged that it is difficult to find and is therefore ignored by humans—and bees.

Other species stagger their productive periods: some dandelions 'open' at nine a.m.; fireweed and red clover around one p.m., and so on. Many species do, of course, bloom simultaneously, but the flowering time between spring and fall is divided more or less equally so that all may be fertilized.

These marvels open up fascinating areas of fact far stranger than fiction, but the point at issue is clear: flower and insect behavior are linked. They have evolved in response to each other to the point that the structure of the flower is such that an exchange of pollen is ensured by the structure and behavior of the insect seeking food.

I have striven to avoid generalizations, which are often wrong, and over-simplification, but in a non-textbook such as this there is always the danger that omission by compression may create confusion. With this in mind and in view of the emphasis I have placed on the biological clock process, I would like to stress that other factors can also be involved as regulating devices to ensure survival of a species.

Atmospheric changes, for instance. In cold or foggy weather, California poppies may not open at all. Culti-vated crocuses may 'hold back' during an exceptionally cold spring; but if the cold persists into early summer the spring flowers will bloom nevertheless. The reason is the length of the day, or rather the increased duration of daylight hours. That is readily understandable, but what is so wonderful in nature is exemplified in the reverse situation, namely that insufficient hours of daylight pre-clude the blooming of spring flowers in January, regardless of how unseasonably warm the weather might be.

Well, we know now that insects are motivated by their molecular clocks, which tell them when to get moving. But they don't just take off and fly around aimlessly; they seem to know precisely where they're going. 'Knowing' is not the right word. They are obeying an instinct so powerful that it enables them to detect a specifically attractive species of flower at a distance and among other species. They may be guided by scent or, more usually, by color.

In the long struggle for existence, flowers of necessity have evolved many beautiful shapes, colors, and patterns to attract their pollinators and so perpetuate their species.

When we think of flower pollination we usually think first of bees, so let's single them out.

The color-sense of bees is limited to recognition of yellow, orange, and green, which appear to them as one color, and blue-green, blue, purple, violet and ultra-violet, which also appear as one color. Preference, or better discrimination, is for yellow, blue, and purple. Bees are blind to red. (*We* see all colors of the spectrum *except* ultra-violet.)

Having enticed an insect by color or smell a flower then has to supply comforts and conveniences to lure its guest into doing its job. The delicate purple lines—frequently on or leading to a yellow spot—on petals of irises, violets, pansies, and others, or the spots and dots inside foxglove blossoms, are not mere decorations but nectar-pollen guides precisely placed.

If bees are blind to red, how are flowers of this color pollinated? To a bee, a bright red poppy or a dull red clover blossom will appear blue because each reflects ultra-violet rays. For a bee to be interested in a white flower it, too, must reflect these rays; some very pale colored or white flowers that show no markings to the naked eye do so when photographed onto film that is sensitive to ultra-violet light, thus proving the point.

Many flowers are equipped with special landing platforms (some orchids), others have hidden mechanisms to ensure that their particular pollinators become loaded with pollen while feeding on nectar (milkweed, spreading dogbane). Ground-hugging, shade-dwelling flowers must also attract special pollinators (wild ginger, Indian pipe).

Nature was not always so efficient. Before the painfully slow evolution of insect-flower relationships (one of the earliest to evolve such a connection was the magnolia, which appeared about a hundred million years ago), such flowers as existed on the young earth were pollinated at the whim of the wind, as indeed grasses and coniferous trees still are. The method was haphazard and wasteful, and more methodical means evolved over the millenia to ensure perpetuation of the species.

An immeasurable period.

An eternity.

And it is shocking to realize that this triumph of evolution can be wrecked in a single day by chemical sprays.

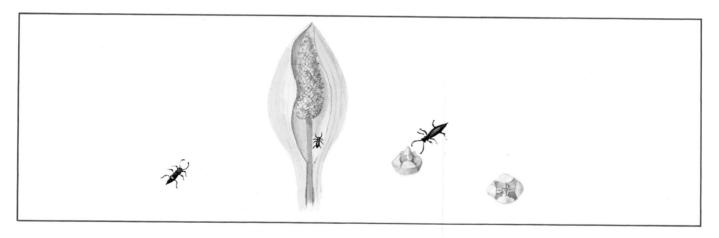

More Than We Ever Wanted to Know About Sex

'A rose is a rose is a rose is a rose,' wrote Gertrude Stein to make a point. That may be forceful writing but it's an offence to botany. There are umpteen species of wild roses (and of course different species of thousands and thousands of other plants) and when we see one our first question is 'What is it called?' To which a botanist will reply in Latin, giving the precise name of that one species, much to the astonishment and admiration of the uninitiated. But you don't have to be a qualified botanist to be able to impress others; anyone can do it. All it requires is study and a lively interest in plants. And the fact that anyone can do it with comparative ease is due to the inspired work of an eighteenth-century enthusiast.

The Linnaean classification system, which ensures foolproof identification, was named after its inventor, Carolus Linnaeus, who, on ennoblement, assumed the name Carl von Linné. Before he tidied things up, every botanist identified plants according to fancy, using such unreliable guides as color, size, and habitat. And as each botanist the world over set his own guidelines and used his own language, which others couldn't understand and which was inexact anyway, the result was predictably chaotic. Linnaeus produced order by simplifying, employing the academically accepted languages of Latin and Greek and, with considerable daring, by using sexual allusions.

The son of a Swedish pastor, Linnaeus was born in 1707. After medical training and a journey of exploration to Lapland in 1732, he established himself, during visits to Germany, Holland, England, and France, as a serious botanist. In 1741 he was appointed Professor of Medicine and Botany at Sweden's famous University of Uppsala, where he remained until his death in 1778.

Although Linnaeus devised a radically new system, his thinking was far from revolutionary. His private life was as prosaic as his career, and like his priestly father he believed firmly in special creation (as described in the Book of Genesis) and the fixity of species. It took Charles Darwin, some one hundred years later, to show that plants (and everything else in nature, including man) evolve towards more perfect adaptation to environment. Darwinism, which upset so many scientific theories of his time, had no effect on the Linnaean system because belief plays no part in it, it being purely and simply a system of classification whereby any plant (and animal) can be identified and slotted into an overall plan. In expounding his system Linnaeus also, almost casually, introduced a method of naming species, which is still used and which, of course, is used throughout this book.

It doesn't sound very exciting, but try to imagine a world without these fundamental tools. Before Linnaeus, naturalists had tried to give specific names incorporating all the distinguishing features of a species. For instance, the humble milfoil labored under the weighty designation *Achillea foliis duplicato-pinnatis gladbris, laciniis linearibus acute laciniatis.* Try to remember that one!

That's bad enough, but the names were constantly being revised and expanded as similar related species came to light. And of course they quite commonly differed from author to author. Linnaeus simplified the whole business by giving each species a name consisting of two Latin words, the first defining the genus and common to every species within that genus, and the second defining the species. He used Latin because it was the custom of the times; it's just as well he did because he wouldn't have made much impact on the world if he had written in his native Swedish.

The masterstroke lay in the separation of the designatory and descriptive functions. The binomial (two-word) system designates the genus and is common to all species within it, followed by the specific name, which describes a single plant in the genus; for instance, *Mimulus lewisii*, *M. alsinoides*, *M. guttatus*—three species in one genus. The simplicity and precision of the system won instant universal acceptance and has endured, pre-Linnaean names having no status in modern scientific literature.

Just for the record, Linnaeus was not the first to devise a classificatory system; the first was Aristotle (384–322 BC) and several others followed suit over the centuries. For example, one Kaspar Bauhin (1560–1624) recorded some 6,000 species, many binomially, in one book, which was of value to Linnaeus as late as 1730.

But Linnaeus's system—division into classes, then subdivision into orders, then orders into genera, and finally genera into species—is the only one that was so carefully worked out and is so widely applicable and easy to use that it has stood the test of time, requiring only certain additions (phylum, family, and sub-species).

As I said earlier, sexing is the key to the system. Linnaeus divided all flowering plants into twenty-three classes based on their male organs, with a twenty-fourth class, the Cryptogamia, covering all plants that seemed to be flowerless, such as the mosses. These classes were then subdivided into orders based on the female organs. In this way, a lily, having six stamens and one stigma, would be placed in the class Hexandria (six men), order Monogynia (one woman). It's such a simple system that anyone with the elementary knowledge to identify the sexual parts of a flower can easily find its place in the Linnaean scheme, particularly because plants that resemble each other in the number and arrangement of their sexual parts usually resemble each other in many other ways as well.

Naturally, some were offended, such as Johann Siegesbeck, a prudish St Petersburg academician. He called Linnaeus's system 'loathsome harlotry' and let it be known that 'God never would, in the vegetable kingdom, have allowed such odious vice as that several males (anthers) should possess one wife (pistil) in common, or that a true husband should, in certain composite flowers, besides its legitimate partner, have near it illegitimate mistresses.' Linnaeus retaliated by giving the name *Siegesbeckia* to a particularly ugly, stinking weed. An English clergyman, who held that a literal translation of the first principles of Linnaean botany was enough to shock female modesty, took some comfort in the belief that virtuous students might not be able to make out the similitude of *Clitoria*.

But by and large, people in the eighteenth century were, fortunately, fairly broadminded, which is something no one can say about the mid-Victorians who, when the craze for natural history swept Britain, were aghast at what young ladies were reading. Darwin's theory of evolution was bad enough in all conscience, for it hit at human pride, but Linnaeus had struck at modesty, and to a Victorian that was far worse.

One must admit they had a point, for the romantic Linnaeus had become so carried away by his sexual system that he rather tactlessly emphasized its metaphorical possibilities. He referred to the Monandria as 'one husband in a marriage', the Diandria as 'two husbands in the same marriage', and the wildly exciting Polyandria as 'twenty males or more in the same bed with the female'. The flowerless plants he named cryptogams or 'clandestine marriages'. In case you think I am making this up, let me quote you a passage from Linnaeus's undergraduate thesis (*Praeludia Sponsaliarum Plantarum*), in which he made his first statement of his system and made plant reproduction wildly erotic:

'Words cannot express the joy that the sun brings to all living things.... Yes, Love comes even to the plants. Males and females, even the hermaphrodites, hold their nuptials (which is the subject that I now propose to discuss), showing by their sexual organs which are males, which females, which hermaphrodites.... The actual petals of a flower contribute nothing to generation, serving only as the bridal bed which the great Creator has so gloriously prepared, adorned with such precious bed-curtains, and perfumed with so many sweet scents in order that the bridegroom and bride may therein celebrate their nuptials with the greater solemnity. When the bed has thus been made ready, then is the time for the bridegroom to embrace his beloved bride and surrender himself to her.'

This madly anthropomorphic passage would no doubt astonish the average bee, which has never looked at nectar-gathering in quite that way. But despite the scru-

ples of their menfolk, Victorian ladies took the whole thing in stride and in numerous books and handbooks expressed with gratitude their obligation to the naturalist who had made the study of botany so delightful and so easy. One lady—a Mrs Jane Marcet—even went so far as to write a book about botany for children in which the following dialogue occurs:

EDWARD: When I have examined a plant, Mamma, how am I to find out its name?

MOTHER: Before you can do so, you must learn how the vegetables that are known have been arranged; and I will explain to you, as clearly as I can, the system of Linnaeus....

And so young Edward is introduced into the exciting world of clandestine marriages and 'twenty males or more in the same bed with the female'.

It's heady stuff, isn't it? But it's nice to know that even the Victorians accepted the fact that *Deus creavit, Linnaeus disposuit.*

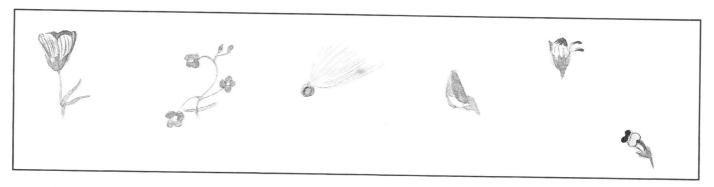

Classification and Naming

Understanding helps insight which in turn simplifies, and for this reason even the novice should know something about plant names. Have no fear, I have no intention of burdening you with a mass of technicalities. My proposition includes three of several categories into which plants are placed: family, genera (singular *genus*, Latin for class or race), and species. Let's take each in turn.

Family. This consists of plants grouped because of certain structural arrangements (principally to do with the flower) that are the same or similar. The family name, which will end in —*aceae* or, exceptionally, *-ae*, is usually based on that of a particular plant typical of the group; thus *Rosa* (rose) is in the family *Rosaceae*. That sounds straightforward enough; but I must point out that the similarities are not always apparent to a non-botanist. As an extreme example—and just to show you how complicated things can get—let's take the family *Rosaceae*. This happens to be a large family that includes such diverse plants as trees and small herbs and encompasses such

things as apples, pears, and strawberries. The common feature is a five-petalled flower, but, just to confuse us, all five-petalled flowers are not necessarily in the rose family!

Genus. This consists of plants that have a family resemblance but differ from each other in subsidiary characteristics. As well as being invaluable, genus names are often great fun. As they reflect the long history of botany— more than 2,000 years—many curious names evolved, as you might expect. Most are descriptive, some are fanciful, many are anything but systematic, and some are suggestive of some dear old gentleman wandering about, absent-mindedly choosing names at random—such as *Ranunculus* for the buttercup genus, so named because some members of the genus grow in or near water where frogs abound (Latin *rana*—frog). That such far-fetched but charming names have endured through the centuries is somehow rather nice and comforting. It happens with common names, too: some of these have survived intact for nearly a thousand years.

Anyway, however fanciful or peculiar botanical names may be, just remember that *all scientific plant names start with the generic name.* Think of it as a surname.

Species. This identifies an assemblage of plants within a genus, based on individual *differences.* In other words, the species name is an adjective specifically describing a plant in order to distinguish it from another species in the same genus, just as children share a family name but are distinguished by individual given names, only the order is reversed. Whereas we refer to a person by his given name followed by his family name (John Doe), in botany the family (meaning generic) name comes first (*Rosa nutkana*): only the generic name is capitalized, no matter to whom or what the specific name may refer.

When a botanist discovers a group of plants not precisely like any others in the same species, he adds another adjective after the specific name with the abbreviation 'var.', for variety. You can see this at the top of the page in many places in this book.

Botanically experienced readers may wonder why I have included such basic facts as these. The answer is twofold. Firstly, far too many books wrongfully assume that such elementary information is common knowledge; and secondly, without it some readers would be puzzled by the formula heading on each page of my text (or other texts). In fact, before leaving the subject I think it might prove helpful to give a simple analysis of a page heading, and for this purpose I have chosen two plants that appear to be completely dissimilar but actually belong to the same family: Yarrow and Canada Thistle.

ENGLISH NAME	FAMILY		BOTANICAL NAME	
	English	Latin	Generic Name	Specific Name
YARROW	Composite	COMPOSITAE	*Achillea*	*millefolium* L.
CANADA THISTLE	Composite	COMPOSITAE	*Cirsium*	*arvense* (L.) Scop.

The initial L. and the abbreviation Scop. refer to the botanists who named the plant or added to its description. The L. stands for Linnaeus, and Scop. for the Italian botanist Giovanni Scopoli.

These details are quoted in serious works so that a name may be traced back to its origin. The specific name is not capitalized in most modern works, even if it is that of a man or a country. A merciful simplification has been adopted by which a genus, once named on a page, is abbreviated to its initial followed by its descriptive adjective of species in the same genus: thus by taking the Canada thistle above and describing another thistle with it, *Cirsium* is simply stated as *C. arvense*, the second thistle being perhaps the wavy thistle, which becomes *C. undulatum.*

From time to time a new plant is discovered that does not fit into any of the accepted slots. Then a family, genus, or species may be created.

Plant names are up-dated more rapidly than the books and dictionaries that list them, and confusion sometimes arises in the use of synonyms. Plants renamed for greater accuracy will have the old name in older books. Really authoritative modern reference works list synonyms as well. The names in this book are as current as the most recent published authorities, but to avoid confusion for the general reader I have not included synonyms.

All you need to remember now is *family, genus,* and *species.*

Enough of this preamble; now let us look at some flowers. As I said earlier, you will find that I have arranged them according to color. While this is neither scientific nor foolproof, it is perhaps the most useful way since color is generally the first impression we have of an unknown plant and is therefore a ready way of finding it in a book. So we start with the white.

WHITE

Achillea millefolium L.

COMPOSITAE

YARROW Composite Family

OTHER NAMES *Milfoil, Tansy, Thousand-leaf, Nosebleed*
HEIGHT *6″–2′/15–60 cm*
HABITAT *Dry sunny locations, open bluffs, roadsides, fields, sea and
        lakeshores*
SEASON *B.C. west coast—April–October; elsewhere—June–August*

The white (sometimes tinged with pink) flat-topped flower-heads of yarrow offer their faces to the sun across most of temperate North America from sea-level in B.C. to altitudes above timberline, across the prairies (as far north as Churchill, Manitoba), and onwards to the east coast. Ringing each flower-cluster are tiny ($5/16$″/8mm) complete (fertile) florets with a two-notched lip at the top of the tube. These are the ray flowers. The disk florets in the center have five evenly spaced short teeth. Ray and disk flowers are therefore somewhat different in appearance from some of their relatives, such as chicory (page 164) or dandelion (page 86). There is considerable variation in the degree of dissection in the feathery gray-green leaves, from which comes one of the common names meaning 'thousand leaves' (French *mille*—thousand, and *feuilles*—leaves).

Alphabetically first in the great composite family, which includes sunflowers and dandelions, the botanical name comes from the Greek Achilles, he of the vulnerable heel. Homer's *Iliad* contains the legend that Chiron, wisest of the centaurs and skilled in medicine, advised Achilles to make an ointment from yarrow to heal his soldiers' wounds after the siege of Troy. The herb is still used to make a tea, alone or with elder flowers and peppermint, as a remedy against the onset of a cold. Dried and powdered, it is mixed with comfrey and plantain to stop nosebleed—hence another of its common names. North-west coast Indians used the leaves to poultice the chest for colds, and chewed them for sore throats. If cows are forced by starvation to eat it, their milk tastes disagreeably of this strongly aromatic plant.

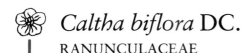 *Caltha biflora* DC.

RANUNCULACEAE

MARSH MARIGOLD Buttercup Family

OTHER NAMES *White-flowered Marigold, Twin-flowered Marigold, Broad-leaved Marigold*
HEIGHT *6"–7"/15–18 cm*
HABITAT *Wet mountain meadows, often beside snowbanks, almost submerged in snow meltwater*
SEASON *May–August*

This very common flower has no petals, only sepals (5–12) which look like them (petaloid). Its blossoms are usually in pairs, which do not necessarily open simultaneously. The kidney-shaped (reniform) leaves are typical of all marsh marigolds, making them easy to identify even if there are no flowers present.

The flower illustrated is found in all the mountain regions of B.C., and north to Alaska, south to California, east to Idaho, Utah, and Colorado.

A similar white (sometimes pink) species (*C. natans*) is found floating or rooted in mud in woodland lakes and slow streams in boreal forest areas of Alberta, Saskatchewan, and Manitoba. *C. palustris* is a yellow, buttercup-like marigold (or Mary's gold) common in slightly moving water in southern Manitoba, eastern and northern Saskatchewan, and forest swamps and meadows of Alberta. A yellow species is also found in coastal bogs in B.C.

Caltha is Latin for plant, mentioned by P. Vergilius Maro, a poet who died in 19 BC. It has been assumed by some authorities that he was referring to the common yellow marigold. The family name *Ranunculaceae* is apt: it comes from the diminutive of *rana*—a frog; several members of the family, including the one illustrated, grow in places frequented by small frogs. Buttercups are another example (see page 80).

Chrysanthemum leucanthemum L.

COMPOSITAE

OX-EYE DAISY Composite Family

OTHER NAMES *Marguerite, Moon-daisy*
HEIGHT *12"–2'/30–60 cm*
HABITAT *Wasteland, fields, sunny slopes, roadsides*
SEASON *June–July*

Low-altitude open places become snowy with the brilliant white petals of this common plant introduced from Europe and now widely naturalized in the northern half of North America. The name should not be confused with that of the yellow *heliopsis*: ox-eye or false sunflower.

Ox-eye daisy is one of the four parents of the popular garden perennial Shasta daisy (*C. maximum*), which also grows wild west of the Cascade Mountains.

Blooming as it does in huge masses and propagating both by seed and root-runner, ox-eye daisy will withstand picking and is, in fact, considered by some western farmers to be a somewhat noxious weed whose presence indicates an acid, impoverished pasture soil. To the wildflower lover, however, a field of the yellow-centered flowers turning towards the sun makes a lighthearted contribution to a summer's day.

As a postscript it must be said that this pretty daisy is a noxious weed only in certain circumstances. Although ox-eye daisies covering twenty per cent of a wheat field will overwhelm it, one per cent is a good sign: the grain will grow better than if no daisies were present. For this information I am indebted to the essay 'Grass' by Vladimir Soloukin of the USSR, but it belongs to peasant lore everywhere, as does the affinity of blue corn flowers with rye, in the same proportions.

The inset shows a longitudinal section of the flower with ray florets on the outer rim of the receptacle and disk florets in the center.

Claytonia lanceolata **Pursh**

PORTULACACEAE

SPRING BEAUTY Purslane Family

OTHER NAME *Lance-leaf Spring Beauty*
HEIGHT *2″–6″/5–15 cm*
HABITAT *Sagebrush foothills to alpine slopes*
  6,000′–7,000′/1,800–2,100 m
SEASON *May–July*

In spite of pink lines on the petals, spring beauty appears white from a distance, and a meadow covered with these little flowers looks snowy. It is somewhat dwarfed in its higher habitat and naturally blooms later than at lower elevations, thus accounting for the apparently long 'spring' reaching into July.

As you can see from the illustration, spring beauty grows from a corm that looks neatly balled and burlapped. As fresh green shoots emerge after the snow begins to melt, black and grizzly bears dig for the edible corms, which have a sweet, nutty flavor. In May and June families of interior B.C. and north-western great plains Blackfoot Indians would in earlier times converge to dig the little spuds in vast quantities (they were known as Indian potatoes). There is a widening interest now among white people in natural foods, but that indefatigable wild-food hunter, Euell Gibbons, in *Stalking the Wild Asparagus*, begs us to take only the largest corms and to replant the others to continue their cycle. Only when a field of spring beauty is threatened with destruction may the corms be dug with a clear conscience.

The flower illustrated grows from B.C. to Saskatchewan, through the Cascade and Olympic Mountains, south to the northern half of the Sierra Nevada and north-west California, eastward to Wyoming and New Mexico. A closely related species (*C. caroliniana*) is found in Manitoba; it may be white or pink with deeper stripes on the petals.

Clintonia uniflora (Schult.) Kunth.

LILIACEAE

QUEEN'S CUP Lily Family

OTHER NAMES *Blue-bead, Bead Lily*
HEIGHT *4″–6″/10–15 cm*
HABITAT *Moist coniferous woods of mountain regions*
SEASON *May–August*

This fragile but quite common lily grows in the mountainous regions of southern Alaska, B.C., south-western Alberta, Washington, Oregon, Montana, and Idaho.

The single flower rises between two or three long slender leaves; occasionally one may see two flowers on a stem. The underground part is a rhizome from which shoots arise at intervals. The blooming season varies according to altitude (the higher the later), so all summer long there are queen's cups in flower somewhere in mountain woods, their wax-white tepals contrasting sharply with surrounding greens, with a bonus in the form of a subtle perfume.

Before 1915 queen's cup had no English name. This was remedied by Julia Henshaw in *Wild Flowers of the North American Mountains*, now, alas, out of print. The generic name commemorates DeWitt Clinton (1769–1828), governor of New York and a well-known botanist.

Bella Coola Indians call blue-bead 'berry of the wolf'. They once regarded it literally as a sight for sore eyes, both berry and leaves being toasted and used as a poultice for eye soreness as well as for cuts.

In Manitoba one may find a very pretty yellow-flowered species (*C. borealis*), also with a blue berry. It grows in deep woods and blooms from May to June.

Convolvulus sepium L. var.
fraterniflorus Mack. & Bush

CONVOLVULACEAE

WHITE MORNING GLORY Convolvulus Family

OTHER NAME *Hedge Bindweed*
HEIGHT *Twining vine either prostrate or climbing*
HABITAT *Roadsides, waste places, hedgerows, ditches*
SEASON *June–August*

'Heaven be thankit!' exclaimed an old farmer, far from his native Herefordshire, when he was told that white morning glory could not stand the cold of Canada's mountains or the far north. It can and does thrive just about anywhere else, from damp ditches to dry crevices in city concrete—indeed, self-sown, it may grace a drab chain-link fence or a naked telephone pole.

This is one of the courtesans of the plant world—beautiful, and *bad*! It was introduced from Europe and became a pervasive weed, to the dismay of farmers and gardeners. For sheer beauty the trumpet-shaped flower, up to 3½″/9 cm across, is hard to beat. Color varies from pure white to pink, or faintly striped. 'All the mornin' glory on the fence' goes the song, and this is it, twining itself inextricably on fence or living plant. Its clasp is not as lethal as that of honeysuckle, which causes great welts and swellings in tree trunks as the living tissues protest the stranglehold. Rather it kills by smothering.

Convolvulus sepium has a smaller relative, field bindweed (*C. arvensis*), which is an even greater menace. Once established in a garden, it is almost impossible to eradicate. Both species put down deep, thick white rhizomes and no matter how far you dig there always seem to be more.

White morning glory is trans-continental (except in the far north and mountains). It sometimes grows in company with poison ivy.

Convolvo means 'to twine' and *sepium* is from *saepes*—hedges or fences, which makes the botanical name very precise indeed.

Cornus canadensis L.

CORNACEAE

DWARF DOGWOOD Dogwood Family

OTHER NAMES *Bunchberry, Dwarf Cornel, Crackerberry*
HEIGHT *3"–7"/7.5–18 cm*
HABITAT *Moist to wet woods, meadows, and bogs; sea level to about 8,000'/2,400 m*
SEASON *May–August*

While it has not been possible to include B.C.'s floral emblem because flowering dogwood is a tree and this book covers flowering herbs, this delightful miniature serves almost as well; it is a replica of its tall and stately relative of the forest. One may come upon a rotten log over which flows a mantle of dazzling white star-like flowers, close packed, a few inches high—beauty with a slightly impish quality. Yet the 'flowers' are not flowers at all but bracts; the true flower head is the central button-like disk.

When the white bracts fall, the central flowers (each with four purplish petals, four stamens, and a straight pistil) become the bunched, bright red berries that account for one of the plant's names and which, with the highly colored leaves that light the autumn woods, are shown in the illustration. Native Indians once ate the berries raw; they are still sought by ruffed grouse, as are the leaves in summer.

The genus includes some spectacular cultivated species such as the eastern pink dogwood and those with variegated leaves, which adorn many of the streets of Victoria, B.C.

Bunchberry is widespread over most of Canada (its specific name means Canadian) and is found also from Alaska south in the mountains to California and New Mexico, and in Minnesota and Pennsylvania. The keen gardener may safely remove a small portion of delicate rooted stem with plenty of humus, acid sphagnum moss, or rotted wood. Given a shady spot, a mulch of pine needles, and sufficient moisture, this small woodland jewel will give years of pleasure.

Cypripedium passerinum Richards.

ORCHIDACEAE

SPARROW'S-EGG LADY'S-SLIPPER Orchid Family

OTHER NAMES *Small White Northern Lady's-slipper, Franklin's
Lady's-slipper, Purple-spot White-slipper*
HEIGHT *6"–12"/15–30 cm*
HABITAT *Mossy woods, wet coniferous humus, lake-margins, borders
of streams, gravel outwashes, and talus slopes*
SEASON *June–July*

This small-flowered orchid was first discovered on one of Sir John Franklin's Arctic expeditions and named *passerinum* because of its slight resemblance to the sparrow's egg (Latin *passer*—a sparrow). In comparison with other orchids, this one looks a little unbalanced with its white pouch set atop a stem up to a foot high, somewhat dwarfed by its comparatively large, ridged leaves, which grow in clasping pairs. Because it grows in surroundings both wet and cold from melted snow, the blooms may remain fresh for several weeks, as though in cold storage. The leaves are hairy (pubescent) and the flower is fragrant. The inset depicts the flower as it begins to fade, the magenta spots blurring until much of the pouch appears purple. Such color changes in white flowers occur frequently.

This orchid may be found in association with mountain avens (page 56) near Jasper, in the Alberta foothills, northern B.C., and elsewhere, being almost transcontinental in distribution.

Another species with a white lip veined with purple is *C. montanum*, which has dark green or deep maroon petals and sepals. You may find this one in the mountains of south-western Alaska, B.C., and Alberta west to Saskatchewan, and south to California, Montana, Wyoming, and Idaho.

Wild orchids are always a thrill to find; one does not expect to see anything so exotic outside a florist's display window. They will die if they are moved from their natural habitat, and are best left alone for others to enjoy.

Drosera anglica Huds.

DROSERACEAE

LONG-LEAVED SUNDEW Sundew Family

OTHER NAMES *None*
HEIGHT *1½″–3″/3.8–8 cm in prairie provinces; 5″–7″/13–18 cm in B.C.*
HABITAT *Bogs and cold swamps*
SEASON *May–August*

This is a flesh-eating plant. True, you almost need a magnifying glass to find it and when you do you may wonder why such an insignificant flower is illustrated here. For once, it is not the flower but the leaves that are interesting.

The green leaves bear marginal, red, modified hairs with little blobs at their tips, each a gland exuding a clear sticky fluid. Small flying insects, attracted to the bright red tentacles, become entangled in their gummy grip; the strangling threads gradually fold inwards to the face of the leaf and the hapless little beast is *digested* by the plant. Tough luck for a beneficial insect that pollinates the sundew and yet is destroyed by it. Why? The sloppy swamp lacks minerals for which the plant must compensate by extracting nutrients from live insects, much as raptorial birds obtain theirs from small animals. The bird regurgitates unwanted roughage; the sundew sucks its victim's juices, then the incurled leaf opens and the drying skeleton is eventually blown away.

Darwin (*The Origin of Species*), discovered in 1875 that the sticky tentacles responded to a touch by a speck of meat or a minute bit of human hair, but did so hardly at all for something inorganic like a pebble. Try it.

Sundews are found, sometimes in magnificent red patches, in all the western provinces, across Canada, and in fact around the northern hemisphere. The species illustrated is fairly widespread in England, which accounts for its specific name. It has a pseudonym, *D. longifolia*, which more accurately describes the species with its long leaves. The commonest sundew is *D. rotundifolia* with round leaves growing flat on the ground. Another, *D. linearis*, has leaves up to 3″/8 cm long. A truly astonishing little plant and easily recognizable.

The generic name comes from a Greek word meaning dew, referring to the shining droplets on the leaf-hairs.

Erythronium oregonum Applegate

LILIACEAE

EASTER LILY Lily Family

OTHER NAMES *White Fawn-lily, Dog-toothed Violet, White Trout Lily*
HEIGHT *5″–9″/13–23 cm*
HABITAT *Woodland and high open shade, open grassland, rock crevices*
SEASON *March–May*

Wildflowers grow where it suits them. It suits this particular lily to grow only in the southern coastal region of B.C., including Vancouver Island, and in western Washington and northern Oregon, the latter giving the flower its specific name. Despite its restricted distribution, its beauty and popularity demanded its inclusion in this selection.

The illustration shows the flower after pollination, with its tepals curved upwards to reveal the wide, flattened white stamens and bright yellow anthers. This is a signal to pollinating insects not to bother visiting a flower that has already been fertilized and so is devoid of nectar, thus saving the insect time and effort. It is not for nothing that growers of orchids go to great lengths to prevent insects from having access to their expensive blooms: they would wither rapidly once they had been pollinated.

But to return to the Easter lily. From one to three blooms per stem is common; more than that is possible, but rare. When conditions are suitable, always around Easter time, this lovely flower grows in profusion. The sight of an area carpeted with the entrancing white flowers is breathtaking and a lift to the spirit after a long winter. Although the flower is protected in many places, some people cannot resist the temptation to pick. And those same people, who 'adore wildflowers', are surprised at how few lilies there are when they return the following year. If they had picked only the flower it would have been bad enough, but usually the leaves are taken also, and of course the bulb, buried deep underground, relies on those two handsome purple- or green-mottled leaves for its nourishment. And so no leaves, no food supply, no flower—at least for a couple of years or so. Should the leaves be taken from the same plant again, the bulb gives up the unequal struggle and dies.

The attempt to transplant an Easter lily to the home garden is not only a fool's game but bulb-snatching from the wild is strictly a 'no-no' for reasons I have emphasized in preface and text. The small bulb lies about a foot deep (30 cm) in hard dry soil and damages easily, and because the above-ground parts are inevitably broken during digging, the plant is certain to die anyway.

Left to itself, the Easter lily performs splendidly. Like many members of the family, the lily's bulb produces bulblets (see chocolate lily on page 226) as well as seeds, the latter being contained in a capsule that stands

upright on the flower-stem. May you take seeds? Well, yes. But it takes three to six years for a seedling to reach flowering age and then only if conditions are perfect. If you want our native erythroniums very badly, try commercial nurseries specializing in wild plants.

If, some Easter time, you are anywhere near one of the habitats mentioned here, it will pay you to make an effort to feast your eyes on an expanse of these gorgeous lilies, for verily Solomon in all his glory was not arrayed like one of these.

For the avid gardener there is still hope in the form of a charming dwarf alpine (*E. dens-canis*) from the Spanish Pyrenees Mountains. While somewhat less spectacular than the North American species, it is easier to grow and therefore merits description here. The tiny narrow whitish bulbs lie but a few inches below the soil where they multiply easily year by year. Each sends up a pair of gray-green leaves mottled with purplish-brown, and a single mauve-green stem about four inches (10 cm) tall, topped by a delicate pink-tepalled bloom. In my wild garden it thrives in sunlight in good loam with added sand for sharp drainage—a must for most bulbs. This is the only European species in the genus and possibly gave its name 'dog-tooth violet' (Latin *dens*—tooth, and *canis*—dog) to the several North American species, although it is still inaccurate: the genus bears no relationship to violets and the likening of the bulbs to dogs' teeth is pretty far-fetched!

E. dens-canis is available from commercial wildflower nurseries. As with other wildflowers propagated commercially for specialist gardeners, the bulbs are fairly expensive. You have to remember that you need only two or three for your initial investment to pay off a hundredfold, not just in quantity but in the excitement of seeing the first shoot appear in spring, continuing through the joy of watching the bud unfold, to pollination and the setting of seed for you to play with next year. *E. dens-canis* is an early bloomer; you can expect it about March or early April at sea level, later in the mountains.

By the way, the word *erythronium* comes from the Greek *erythro*— red. This refers to *E. dens-canis* just described but also applies to *E. revolutum*, a bright pink North American *erythronium* which, except for its color, looks exactly like the white lily illustrated here. The specific name indicates that the tepals recurve as they mature. These two lilies grow in different habitats: the white prefers the dry summer soil of open mossy woodlands or meadows, whereas the pink grows well only in the fine dark sandy soil associated with winter-flooded valleys. The pink is not common; Vancouver Island boasts possibly the only extensive area carpeted with pink blooms in breathtaking profusion. I have patiently grown it from seed, enjoyed a few meager flowers for two years—and then nothing. It just does not seem possible to duplicate its normal environment and I have given up trying to compete with nature.

Fragaria virginiana **Duchesne**

ROSACEAE

WILD STRAWBERRY Rose Family

OTHER NAMES *None*
HEIGHT *3"–4"/7.5–10 cm*
HABITAT *Open woodland, rocky bluffs, roadsides*
SEASON *May–June*

If you have found this small member of the rose family in bloom, remember to return a month later for the sweet, fragrant fruits. They make better eating (if you can ever find enough) than the cultivated ones. Since the plant increases by stolons (horizontal surface stems) there is no harm in picking the fruit carrying the seeds.

Several species grow across vast areas from Alaska to California, east to the Atlantic coast, and in Colorado and Georgia. The differences between them are small and all can easily be identified. The species illustrated possesses two characteristics worth noting: in spring the leaves are blue-green, and the tooth at the tip of each leaflet is smaller than those flanking it. Occasionally you may see a six-petalled flower on the same plant as those with typical five petals. Compare the wild strawberry with the cinquefoils (pages 76, 78) for the similarity of the flowers and differences in the leaves—yet all are 'roses'.

Naturally Indian people relish wild strawberries. Squirrels adore them and it takes luck to beat them to a patch of ripe fruit. The whole plant has medicinal value and I have used it successfully to treat diarrhea in infant animals. Strawberry and stonecrop leaves, made into an infusion, are a specific remedy for this distressing and often fatal condition.

Strawberries are so named because they 'strew' or 'straw' the ground with their stolons. Wild strawberries have been on record for more than 900 years and were known to the Anglo-Saxons as 'streowberies'.

Goodyera oblongifolia Raf.

ORCHIDACEAE

RATTLESNAKE PLANTAIN Orchid Family

OTHER NAMES *Large Rattlesnake Orchid, Lattice-leaf*
HEIGHT *10"–15"/26–38 cm*
HABITAT *Cool, mossy woods*
SEASON *June–September*

A flamboyant flower is often surrounded by modest leaves, but here the reverse is true. The single straight stem bears small greenish-white flowers (sometimes on one side, sometimes spirally as in the illustration), which may pass unnoticed but for the striking rosette of rich green and white mottled leaves at its base, cushioned in soft mosses. The irregular checkerboard design is due to the absence of chlorophyll in the white parts. *Oblongifolia* (Latin *oblongus*—oblong) refers to the leaves, in which there may be a good deal of variation, some having merely a white mid-vein, others the random patterns as shown in the illustration. Goodyer was a seventeenth-century English botanist.

Flower-buds in this species require several weeks to emerge from their green hoods, and by the time they open fully the leaves are beginning to grow dull as the mosses into which they are tucked dry out in summer heat.

This orchid has a wide range from Alaska south through B.C. to most of the western United States, east to Saskatchewan and Michigan. A very similar, closely related species (*G. repens*), with clear green leaves and a creeping habit, is found from B.C. to Manitoba, in Alaska and the Rocky Mountains, then south to New Mexico. Neither species is a true plantain and neither is effective against snake-bite as was believed in the eighteenth century, but both contain many of the medicinal virtues of members of the plantain family. A leaf rubbed between the fingers will separate into two halves, whose inner, moist surface soothes mosquito bites, burns, or cuts and scratches.

During confinement Thompson Indian mothers chewed the leaves to ease pain and predict the child's sex. If she could swallow them it would be a boy, but if she couldn't keep them down it would be a girl.

Habenaria dilatata (Pursh) Hook. var.
    leucostachys (Lindl.) Ames

ORCHIDACEAE

FRAGRANT WHITE ORCHID Orchid Family

OTHER NAMES *Tall White Bog Orchid, Rein Orchid*
HEIGHT *2'–3' / 6–9 dm*
HABITAT *Bogs, swamps, soggy meadows, wet stream or lake shores;*
           lowest valleys to 10,000' / 3,000 m
SEASON *June–September*

The orchid family is a large one with about 15,000 species, second only to the composite family, which contains about 20,000 species, yet many people are under the impression that orchids grow only in tropical jungles. In fact, a number of species are native to the cooler climates of North America and Europe. Naturally, the flowers are much smaller than the enormous exotic jungle species familiar in florists' shops; these grow mostly on trees, drawing their sustenance directly from the air; most of our wild orchids grow in the ground, have green leaves, and so produce their food by photosynthesis; some have no green leaves and are saprophytes, living on decayed organic matter.

Orchids are special. They are possibly the most fascinating of all wildflowers. A complete description of their complex structures and highly sophisticated methods of reproduction cannot be attempted in this space, and in any case it is beyond the scope of this book. But a fairly simple explanation of an orchid's parts will aid recognition in the wild; if you are intrigued enough to pursue the subject, consult the references given at the end of this book.

The flower is remarkably symmetrical, being divisible into equal halves from back to front, and often vertically; it forms an equilateral triangle with its three sepals, which are usually the color of the petals, although the third is different in size and shape from the other two and forms the upper center part of the flower. The lip, which serves as a landing strip for insects, may be forked, pouched, or saucer-shaped. In the fragrant white orchid it is a long, narrow tongue, its widened base extending backwards into an equally long tubular nectar spur. Orchids have dispensed with the filaments that in other flowers carry the anthers (male parts) with their pollen visible; instead, the anthers sit flat against the flower's 'throat', rather like tonsils (see inset, bottom). The pollen, in tiny clusters known as pollinia, is inside the anthers and by means of an extraordinary series of timed triggering mechanisms becomes attached to the legs, head, or back of a visiting insect, which has to work hard to force its way past the anthers to the nectar.

When these complicated processes have come to fruition as seeds, one further ingredient must be present to complete the miracle of creation. The seeds must be penetrated by the microscopic threads of a specific species of fungus and until this takes place, the seeds cannot germinate. There are several *million* seeds in a single capsule and if even a small percentage reached maturity, orchids would be very common flowers. As it is, so few encounter ideal conditions that orchids are still wonderful rarities.

The generic name *habenaria* is from the Latin *habenas*—rein or strap; this refers to the long spur and lip and accounts also for one of the common names for this stately bog orchid, which has the added attraction of being heavily perfumed. The specific name *dilatata* means 'expanded', describing the widened portion of the lip.

The top inset shows a partly opened flower with undescended lip, the spur visible below it. Next, a mature flower with its twisted ovary. The enlarged anther sacs below have already been mentioned.

The fragrant white and several varieties of the species are found in all the western provinces of Canada and throughout the Cascade Mountains to north-west California. Another (*H. saccata*), not quite as tall as the fragrant white, has light green flowers and a shorter spur and is found from north-west California to Alaska.

Wild orchids cannot withstand a radical change of environment and no attempt should be made to transplant them. Growing them from seed requires ideal conditions and monumental patience. Their natural habitats are inexorably disappearing; if future generations are to see these beautiful flowers in the wild we must control the urge to pick or dig, contenting ourselves with sketch pad or camera.

Heracleum lanatum Michx.

UMBELLIFERAE

COW PARSNIP Parsley Family

OTHER NAMES *Indian Rhubarb, Cow-cabbage, Masterwort,*
Hercules-parsnip
HEIGHT *6'–12'/1.82–3.7 m*
HABITAT *Rich, damp soil of roadside ditches*
SEASON *Late May – early July*

The Herculean proportions of this plant ensure its visibility from car or train; it is possibly the largest perennial in the west. The central flower-head may be 15"/39 cm in diameter, flanked by two smaller ones. The base of each flower-stem is clasped by an off-white, balloon-like sheath that tapers to a tuft of green leaves; basal leaves are hairy beneath, each leaf having three large leaflets, coarsely toothed and lobed, and each being up to 12"/30 cm long. Stems are ridged, hairy, and hollow. A huge canvas would be needed to do justice to this structure; the illustration here gives but an impression, with insets to show the detail of front-row flowers and the shapely fruits, each with two to four visible oil tubes. Of about sixty species, this is the only true North American native, and while it will produce mature plants from seed in about three years, it's a bit big for a small garden.

Heracleum is widespread in North America and very common in the west—so much so that Parsnip River in northern B.C. is named for the quantities of the plant growing along its banks.

Wild and domestic animals forage for the leaves in spring, and it is safe for humans, being a favorite green vegetable of all Indian peoples of the west. Leaf and bud stems can be peeled and eaten raw or cooked; despite their smell, they taste pleasantly of celery, a relative.

Heracleum is the name of several ancient towns, dedicated to the Greek god Heracles (more familiar by the Roman name of Hercules). *Lanatum* is Latin for woolly—hence lanolin, the oil from sheep's wool.

Important Note: Do not attempt to eat this plant if you are not *absolutely* certain of its precise identity. Deadly poisons are contained in several similar-looking species such as water hemlocks (*Cicuta* spp.) and purple spotted, finely cut-leafed poison hemlock (*Conium maculatum*). All are smaller and less coarse than *Heracleum lanatum*. There is said to be enough poison in a walnut-sized piece of the root of *Cicuta douglasii* to kill a full-grown cow. The Greek philosopher Socrates was sentenced to death by drinking hemlock (*Conium maculatum*). And the plant was immortalized by Keats in his 'Ode to a Nightingale':

> My heart aches, and a drowsy numbness pains
> My sense, as tho' of hemlock I had drunk . . .

Ledum groenlandicum Oeder

ERICACEAE

LABRADOR-TEA Heath Family

OTHER NAMES *Hudson's Bay Tea, Indian Tea, Bog Laurel*
HEIGHT *12"–4'/30–120 cm*
HABITAT *Bogs, swamps, swampy woodlands, lakeshores*
SEASON *May–July*

In pioneer days the leaves made a valuable tea substitute or additive to the meager tea rations of hard-working men in the north, and for Indians throughout Canada. To the former it became known as Indian tea and to the latter as Hudson's Bay tea. The leaves have recently been discovered to contain a toxic compound that can induce cramps and paralysis if taken in large doses. However, I frequently drink tea brewed from fresh or dried leaves and consider it one of the most aromatic and refreshing of the wild herbs. Take a heaping teaspoonful of crushed or broken leaves and add to a cup of boiling water, with a little honey if you prefer it sweet.

The specific name places this shrubby plant in Greenland, whence it reaches into Alaska, along the Pacific coast, then inland across the prairies to the north Atlantic states. A very close species (*L. glandulosum* var. *glandulosum*) grows in B.C., east of the Cascade Mountains, through Montana, north Wyoming, central Idaho, and north-east Oregon. Members of the genus look like small rhododendrons, though less showy, the blooms being small and clustered at the tops of the woody stems. The leaves are the most interesting part of the plant. When crushed they give off a sharp, pungently pleasant scent resembling wintergreen. They are leathery in texture with no visible veins on the surface, and the edges are in-rolled, all of which helps to conserve moisture and withstand harsh northern climates. The reverse side of the leaf (see inset) has a visible center vein, partially obscured by thick woolly hairs, white when the leaves are young, red-brown as they age. It looks and feels like felt. Other interesting examples of leaf-structure adapted to fierce winters abound; see mountain avens (page 56).

Maianthemum dilatatum (Wood) Nels. & Macbr.

LILIACEAE

WILD LILY-OF-THE-VALLEY Lily Family

OTHER NAMES *Two-leaved Solomon's Seal, Beadruby, Deerberry, May Lily*
HEIGHT *4″–10″/10–25 cm*
HABITAT *Heavy-rainfall forest*
SEASON *May–July*

When you look down upon an area of forest floor carpeted by this delicate plant, it is the large, heart-shaped, bright green leaves that first attract attention. They are wide, to catch as much light as possible, and shaped to a pointed drip-tip to enable them to shed raindrops onto their roots. The racemes of tiny, wax-white flowers punctuate the multitudinous greens of the leaves like banks of little candles in the forest's dim light, and are almost too small to draw, let alone paint! The flowers give off a faint perfume. In summer the flowers are replaced by shiny green, brown-mottled, semi-translucent berries, which later turn red. They are edible, although not particularly tasty, and were eaten cooked by B.C. coastal Indians.

This charming little lily grows to the west of B.C.'s coastal mountains, north to Alaska, south to California, and east to northern Idaho. A very closely related, similar-looking species (*M. canadense* var. *interius*) grows in Alberta, Saskatchewan, and Manitoba, where it is common and is known as two-leaved Solomon's seal.

Lily-of-the-valley might well be called May lily, since the generic name is Greek: *maios*—May, and *anthemon*—flower. There is a custom in France of giving a bunch of the cultivated lily-of-the-valley (*muguet*) to one's girl-friend on May Day, when the blooms (and the girl?) are at the peak of perfection.

Both lilies will stand transplanting to a damp, shady location in your wild garden, but may become invasive. A bottomless bucket sunk below ground around the plant will prevent this.

Monotropa uniflora L.

MONOTROPACEAE

INDIAN PIPE Indian Pipe Family

OTHER NAMES *Ghost Plant, Corpse Plant, Ice Plant*
HEIGHT *5″–9″/13–23 cm*
HABITAT *Deep gloom of coniferous forests; spruce woods*
SEASON *May–July*

This flower is something of an enigma, well worth studying. First sight of a clump of the translucent, waxy white pipes glimmering in the sunless forest is breathtaking—the plant seems unreal. Its leaves have been modified to mere scale-like bracts that clasp the flower stem alternately from ground level upwards. The flowers, borne one to a stem, rise from the soil as white, ready-made buds, bent sharply downward. As the stem grows, the flower remains bent down in one direction. (*Monotropa* comes from two Greek words: *monos* and *tropos*—one direction; *uniflora* means one-flowered.) Monotropa reaches its full height in the short space of a week. After pollination by such flying insects as frequent the gloomy surroundings, the bell-shaped, inch-long flower rotates upwards until it is erect. The swollen ovary is colored soft salmon pink (normally the plant's only touch of color) and the ten or more anthers are visible. If you are lucky you may come across a rare group where each pipe has a clear pink stem. Sometimes the shading may be mauve, pale blue, or gray, but always the general appearance of the plant is white and fragile. If you touch it, it will turn black, and the whole plant turns black with age. Furthermore, Monotropa does not always appear in the same place each season; it may disappear for several years, reappearing in a different location, sometimes just a few feet from the original group.

Among the living flowers you usually find some of the previous year's brown, woody seed pods, with a few dried bracts adhering to the stems. These may be gently pulled up and used in miniature flower arrangements.

Having no green leaves with which to synthesize its own food—that is, with which to use light energy to convert carbon dioxide and water into sugar—how does Monotropa survive? It was once thought to be a parasite, like the broomrape (page 186), which feeds on the tissues of the roots of leaf-bearing hosts. The rather pithy derivation is from two Greek words: *sitos*—food, and *para*—alongside ('One who eats at the table of another').

When it was realized that Monotropa does not grow on another plant's roots, it was thought to be a saprophyte (Greek *sapro*—putrid, and *phyte*—plant), meaning a plant that feeds on sugars contained in dead organic matter in the soil, as do some fungi. The theory was bolstered by

the fact that Monotropa's roots are surrounded by a species of fungus (a Boletus).

That theory was also shattered, this time by Erik Bjorkman of the Royal School of Forestry in Sweden. He questioned Monotropa's ability to grow so fast in deep shade, without leaves and in poor soil. He made the startling discovery that Monotropa should be returned to its original slot as a parasite.*

It is well known that plants frequently have fungi growing on their roots and Monotropa is no exception; the trees under which it is found also have fungi on their roots. Bjorkman set out to prove that the fungus was the same species on both. He found that although the tree benefits from the fungus and vice versa, they can survive without each other. On the other hand, being unable to absorb energy from the sun or nutrients from the soil, Monotropa is wholly dependent on the fungus, which acts as a bridge between the two. Thus Monotropa is indeed a parasite, deriving its nutrition directly from the fungus and indirectly from the tree roots. It is still, however, listed as a saprophyte in a number of wildflower books.

Because of Monotropa's delicacy and its vital connection with the fungus, it is impossible to transplant.

Monotropa is closely related to the heath family, which includes the arbutus tree. *M. uniflora* is found across Canada, south into north-west California, and from there to the east coast, wherever there is deep humus and dense shade.

Another member of this interesting family, Pinesap (*Hypopitys monotropa*, or *Monotropa hypopitys*, depending on which author you consult), bears a raceme of several flowers varying from pinkish to straw-colored. It, too, turns black with age. Its name is pure Greek: *hypo*—beneath, and *pitys*—pine tree. Like *M. uniflora*, it was classified as a saprophyte but is now, from Bjorkman's conclusions, classed as a parasite. It is found from B.C. to northern California and eastwards to the Atlantic coast.

Thompson Indians named it 'wolf's urine', believing that the plant grew wherever a wolf urinated, one of the more gentle legends pertaining to that much-maligned animal.

The insets in the painting, from top to bottom, show: front and back view of enlarged anther; ten anthers and five-lobed pistil seen from above; ovary and stamens.

*BJORKMAN, Erik 'Monotropa hypopitys L. An Epiparasite on Tree Roots', Physiologia Plantarum, Vol. 13 (1960), pp. 308-27.

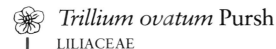
Trillium ovatum Pursh

LILIACEAE

LARGE WHITE TRILLIUM Lily Family

OTHER NAME *Western Wake-robin*
HEIGHT *12"–18"/30–45 cm*
HABITAT *Moist woods*
SEASON *April–May*

Topping up with oil is not an exclusively human activity: as soon as trillium seed-pods burst open, the ants move in to collect the oil-rich seeds. Each seed has a little appendage containing oil, which is eaten by an ant, leaving the seed intact. This is dropped some distance from the parent plant where it may with luck germinate—one of nature's excellent devices for plant dispersal.

When you see an aging trillium for the first time you may be forgiven for thinking it is another species. The dramatic change of color of some white flowers is another of nature's tricks: the flower has been pollinated and the change from white to pink to a dull crimson is a signal to insects not to bother visiting; they need their energy to work blooms that have yet to be fertilized.

Trillium grows from an underground root (rhizome), instead of a bulb like the majority of the lily family; the three petals, three sepals, and thrice-divided stigma are typical of lilies and in this case there are also three large green leaves immediately below the flower, setting it off beautifully.

'If I pick a trillium, will it really take seven years to bloom again?' is a question often asked. Breaking the stem automatically removes the only leaves, and the plant cannot make food for storage in the rhizome for the following season, so that only a spindly little three-leafed shoot will appear. It has been my experience in observing trilliums after depredations by deer and wild rabbits that one must protect a chewed-off plant for at least three years, and even then the bloom will be rather puny. Anyway, why pick them? In the unlikely event that you arrive home with an unwilted flower, how long will it last in a vase? Wildflowers are much shorter-lived than cultivated ones. Take a photograph instead, or try growing a few seeds.

Wake-robin, which takes its name from its early blooming, was for the Thompson Indians an important medication, and only experts were allowed to touch it. They boiled the rhizomes and used the liquid as an eyewash, long before this strikingly handsome plant was reported for the first time in 1806 by Capt. Meriwether Lewis (of the Lewis and Clark expedition), who found it near rapids on the Columbia River.

There are trillium species across Canada in various colors, from the one illustrated and its much larger relative *T. grandiflorum*, also white, to flowers that are yellowish, pink, red, and a rather dirty green. Naturally they cross the border and the illustrated species is found as far south as central California, and east to north-west Colorado and Montana.

Viola canadensis L.

VIOLACEAE

WESTERN CANADA VIOLET Violet Family

OTHER NAMES *None*
HEIGHT *8"–2'/20–60 cm*
HABITAT *Loamy soil of moist woodlands*
SEASON *May–June*

As violets go, this one is very tall; yet when transplanted to a garden it sometimes becomes a ground hugger with short stems spreading rapidly by stolons to the point of becoming invasive. It is a lovely species with many blooms to a plant. The central lower petal has the usual violet family's 'trademark', purple bee-guides; the unusual thing about this particular species is that the two upper petals have delicate purple backs while still appearing white from the front.

This species ranges widely from Alaska through B.C. to Oregon and Arizona, in the Rocky Mountains, and from Alberta to Manitoba.

All violets have medicinal properties, notably as antiseptics and expectorants. Flowers and leaves are used in syrups for coughs and colds, and the lightly boiled leaves contain a mucilage that is an excellent skin softener and hair rinse. A poultice for any skin irritation or wound can be made by pouring boiling water over the leaves and letting them steep for twelve hours, then using the liquid on lint or cotton batting.

Viola is the Latin name for the plant; the specific name is self-evident. There are three more violets in this book with which to make comparisons (see pages 88, 218, 220).

Zigadenus venenosus S. Wats.

LILIACEAE

DEATH CAMAS Lily Family

OTHER NAMES *Poison Camas, Zigadenus, Zygadene, Poison Onion,*
        Meadow Death Camas
HEIGHT *10"–2'/25–60 cm*
HABITAT *Coastal 'prairies'; rocky bluffs wet in spring; grassy hillsides;*
        sagebrush slopes; mountain forest in exposed places
SEASON *May–June*

This plant is dangerous. Two bulbs, raw or cooked, are sufficient to kill
you. It is equally fatal to sheep and cattle, although both are known to eat
the leaves in spring. While the whole plant is poisonous, the greatest concentration lies in the seeds and bulbs. There are three species, and in view
of their toxicity I will describe them separately.

Z. *venenosus* (illustrated) grows in southern B.C. including the south-
eastern portion of Vancouver Island; south to Baja California, east to
Alberta and south-west Saskatchewan, and to the Dakotas, Nebraska, and
Colorado.

Z. *elegans* has broader leaves and a more open flower-head; the
flowers are the same creamy white as the illustrated species. It is found
from Alaska to the interior of B.C., through Washington and eastern Oregon to Nevada and Arizona; in moist meadows in Alberta; in saline meadows in Saskatchewan and southern Manitoba; in Montana; from the
Dakotas to New Mexico. This species is only slightly poisonous to livestock.

Z. *gramineus* is so nearly like the species illustrated it is considered by
some to be but another form of Z. *venenosus*. It is found in southern B.C.
east of the Coast Mountains, through the Okanagan Valley, and in the
Kootenays. It is common in southern Alberta and less common on the Saskatchewan prairie. It is not found in Manitoba. In the U.S.A. it is found in
the Rocky Mountains and Colorado, east Washington, northern Idaho,
and Montana. This species is said to be the deadliest camas of all.

The bulbs look like those of the edible blue camas (page 160) and
could also be confused with other edible bulbs growing in the same places.
Only the flower-color denotes the difference.

YELLOW TO ORANGE

Arnica cordifolia Hook.

COMPOSITAE

HEART-LEAVED ARNICA Composite Family

OTHER NAME *Leopard's Bane*
HEIGHT *8"–2'/20–60 cm*
HABITAT *Moist soil of open woods and areas that have been burned,
         from foothills to 9,000'/2,700 m, especially under quaking
         aspen and ponderosa and lodgepole pines*
SEASON *April–August, occasionally September*

The flower of this plant may be confused with two other members of the family, balsamroot and sunflower, but the leaves are distinctly different, being heart-shaped. The thirty-odd species of *Arnica* bloom a few weeks later than balsamroot or sunflower and the plants are smaller and more slender. The petals are similar, being flowers in their own right—ray florets on the outside and disk florets in the center. Some have no ray florets while others have showy ones like the one illustrated. Ray and disk florets are shown separately. For comparison with the two species mentioned above turn to pages 52 and 60.

Heart-leaved arnica is widely distributed in B.C., Alberta, and Saskatchewan, and a relative (*A. fulgens*) is found on drier soil from the interior of B.C. to the southern prairie of Manitoba; it has narrower leaves and the flower is orange-yellow instead of lemon. *Fulgens* means shining and *cordifolia* means heart-leaved. Both are brilliantly showy plants and can be grown in a woodland garden either from seed or from small pieces of rhizome.

A. cordifolia also ranges from Alaska, the Yukon, and Northwest Territories, southwards via the east side of the Cascade Mountains to the northern California Coast Ranges and New Mexico, as well as in northern Michigan.

The plant is soft in texture and wilts very quickly if picked. It has a characteristic smell (rather than perfume), is aromatic yet bitter to taste, and is probably poisonous. Tincture of arnica is prepared in Europe from the flowers of the alpine *A. montana*, although *A. fulgens* has been found to be pharmaceutically superior. It is valuable applied locally to bruises, but given internally it raises body temperature, and severe, sometimes fatal cases of poisoning are on record.

Balsamorhiza sagittata (Pursh) Nutt.

COMPOSITAE

BALSAMROOT Composite Family

OTHER NAMES *Spring Sunflower, Bigroot, Arrowleaf Balsamroot, Big Sunflower*
HEIGHT *10″–30″/25–75 cm*
HABITAT *Dry hillsides, exposed sunny slopes*
SEASON *B.C.—late April–early July; Alberta, Saskatchewan—May–July*

Here is another of the innumerable instances of misleading common names. Balsamroot is not a true sunflower although it is a member of the same family.

Clumps of balsamroot make a dazzling display of many brilliant flowers rising on single stems above the silver-green, arrow-shaped leaves that characterize this species (*sagittata*—an arrow). The flower-head consists of rays, each of which is a complete flower made up of a tube containing a minute brown pistil. The central disk is filled with tiny flowers, also tubular, in which the style acts as a plunger to push out the pollen. In the illustration the ray floret is life-size and the disk floret is enlarged. Balsamroot is also found in areas throughout Washington, south through the Sierra Nevadas of California, east to western Montana, west South Dakota, and Colorado.

This was an important food-plant for Interior Salish, Kootenay, and Blackfoot Indians. The young tender shoots and bud stems were eaten raw, while the thick resinous roots (Greek *balsamon*—balsam, and *rhiza*—root) were roasted in spring; the oily seeds were mashed into flour. Domestic livestock, horses, and wild deer and elk, among other animals, relish the plant; it has been said that when balsamroot is in bloom the land is ready for grazing. Animals know that the plant is only fit to eat when very young; later in the season cattle, horses, and other animals give it a wide berth.

Balsam is another name for balm, a medicinal gum obtained from certain trees and well-known to peoples in Europe and the Middle East. Balm is mentioned several times in the Old Testament, and in those times it was considered valuable enough to be used as a gift: 'Carry the man . . . a present, a little balm' (Genesis 43:11).

Cypripedium calceolus L. var.
parviflorum (Salisb.) Fern.

ORCHIDACEAE

YELLOW LADY'S SLIPPER Orchid Family

OTHER NAMES *Yellow Moccasin Flower, Golden Slipper, Yellow Noah's Ark, Yellow Indian Shoe*
HEIGHT *6″–12″/15–30 cm*
HABITAT *Moist woodlands and banks, bogs, swamp edges, lake and stream shores*
SEASON *April–July; August in extreme north*

This magnificent orchid is found in all the western provinces and much of eastern Canada and in areas of Washington and Oregon, Wisconsin, Idaho, Wyoming, and Colorado. Sometimes it grows in surprising places such as dry, gravelly soil in full sun beside a highway, although for the most part it prefers the habitat mentioned above. It grows singly or in quite large clumps but is variable as to size, perfume, and the color of the curious strap-like twisted side petals, which may be yellowish, greenish, or purplish brown. The 'slipper', however, is always yellow.

Yellow lady's slipper has a number of medicinal uses listed in a cyclopedia of botanical drugs reissued in 1956 and undoubtedly still in use. The powdered root, under the name Cypripedin, is stated to allay the pain of neuralgia and to promote sleep. People with sensitive skins may experience irritation on touching this species of orchid, which is somewhat hairy. A synonym for the yellow lady's slipper is *C. calceolus* L. var. *pubescens* (hairy). The inflammatory action increases as the plant reaches the seed phase. This may serve as a warning not to touch the plant, which should not in any case be picked; nor can it be transplanted with any hope of success.

The name of Aphrodite, Greek goddess of love and beauty, is linked to the botanical name. She had several names—we know her also as Venus—of which Cypria or Cypris associate her with Cyprus, where she is reputed to have been born; her Greek name was Kupriotes or Kupris. The second half of the generic name comes from the Greek word *pedilon*—a slipper, or Latin *pes*—foot, referring to the yellow pouch. Tautologically, *calceolus* means a small shoe, but who are we to question the enthusiasm of that grand old man of botany Linnaeus (1707–78), whose initial after the specific name signifies that he first named this orchid? The first record of the plant, however, was made in 1640 by John Parkinson, herbalist to King Charles I, more than half a century before Linnaeus was born.

Dryas drummondii Richards.

ROSACEAE

MOUNTAIN AVENS Rose Family

OTHER NAMES *Drummond's Mountain Avens, Yellow Dryad*
HEIGHT *4"–10"/10–25 cm*
HABITAT *Exposed gravel slopes and mountain ridges; river bars and
          flats*
SEASON *Late May – August*

Here is an example of superb adaptation of a mountain plant to its harsh environment. Tough roots hold it safely against the icy blast of high winds; the spreading mats of evergreen leaves (unusual in this family) are waxy, leathery, and slightly rolled under at the edges, with white, woolly undersides, all to conserve moisture in summer and shed ice in winter. Tiny root nodules store nitrogen, which tends to leach out of gravelly soil subject to snow-melt, when the leaves must be ready to produce food for the plant.

Demurely drooping yellow flowers grow just tall enough to attract insects, but never open wide like other flowers. Notice the hairs on the calyx: these are sticky, glandular, and purple, in lovely contrast to the yellow petals. Fluffy seed heads float just above the flowers, even before these are mature. As with clematis, milkweed, and other seeds (achenes), the plumy tails catch the wind and travel long distances to find suitable crevices in which to germinate.

Dryas in Latin and Greek means a wood-nymph, although paradoxically mountain avens thrives only in exposed, sunny locations! There are two other members of the genus (*D. integrifolia* and *D. octopetala*), both mountain plants with white or cream flowers that open wide, like little roses with eight (or seven to nine) petals. The latter is the floral emblem of the Northwest Territories.

Yellow dryad ranges widely in Alaska, the Rocky Mountains south to north-east Wisconsin, in B.C., south to Oregon, and east across Canada and the northern American states.

Erythronium grandiflorum **Pursh**

LILIACEAE

GLACIER LILY Lily Family

OTHER NAMES   *Yellow Avalanche Lily, Snow Lily, Adder's Tongue,*
Dog-tooth Violet, Fawn Lily
HEIGHT   *10"–12"/25–30 cm*
HABITAT   *Rich, moist soil in shaded woods; streambanks; subalpine*
meadows, mountains to timberline
SEASON   *April – mid-August according to elevation*

Erythronium grandiflorum rolls resoundingly from the tongue, and here is
a case where it really does pay to 'have the Latin', since at least one of the
lily's common names is misapplied—it is not a violet, which has a family to
itself. The generic name (Greek *erythros*—red) means that there is red
somewhere in the plant; here it is the anthers, which vary considerably in
color in this species. This one is found only east of the Cascade Mountains; yellow anthers (see inset) and creamy white ones are found up to
12,000'/3,700 m in B.C. in the Rocky Mountains, down to the foothills
of Alberta, in the Olympic Mountains and south to northern Oregon, and
east to Montana, Wyoming, and Colorado. A low-growing, almost dwarf
form with yellow anthers is found in the mountains of Vancouver Island.

The deep-seated bulbs were a valuable food for B.C. Interior Salish
Indians and a Shuswap family might harvest up to 200 lbs/90 kg a year,
which they cooked and ate immediately or threaded and hung to dry for
winter use. Small rodents store them, and black and grizzly bears dig and
eat them fresh. Each bulb dug up means the death of a lily and wholesale
harvesting by humans is fortunately no longer practiced.

As its name implies, the glacier lily pushes its leaf-enfolded buds
through melting snow, or at the edge of receding snow, and reaches its
peak of perfection in early July at about 8,000'/2,500 m. The specific
name means 'large-flowered', but it would seem that *E. oregonum* (page
20) might well have been given the adjective.

Helianthus annuus L.

COMPOSITAE

WILD SUNFLOWER Composite Family

OTHER NAMES *None*
HEIGHT *2'–6'/6–18 dm*
HABITAT *Open areas with medium-moist soil, abandoned fields, waste places, roadsides, and in mountains to 7,000'/2,100 m*
SEASON *July–September*

Nobody seems certain whether this is a garden escape or, conversely, whether it is one of the parents of the enormous domestic sunflower. Does it matter? Wild sunflower is a handsome member of a large genus containing many species and it is found throughout most of Canada and the United States. It is the state flower of Kansas and is cultivated to a limited extent as a forage crop and for the oil in the seeds, used to make cooking oil, margarine, and oil paints. And James Nicholson made a fortune marketing sunflower and other seeds as birdseed—enough to endow the multi-volume *Dictionary of Canadian Biography*!

This versatile plant is useful in other ways: gin and sugar can be added to water in which the seeds have been boiled; this is given in small doses several times a day to relieve laryngeal and pulmonary congestion. Sunflower leaves have been used in the treatment of malaria. Indians made a yellow dye from the flowers and used the fiber from the stems to make string or nets (it is also used in the textile industry). They also knew the value of the oil in the seeds, and of the seeds themselves as food.

Helianthus annuus takes its name from the Greek *helios*—sun (the flower rotates with the sun) and *annuus*—annual (renews itself from seed each year).

One of its many relatives is the so-called Jerusalem artichoke, whose swollen tubers are cooked in North America and Europe as an alternative to potatoes (they have a rather soapy texture and sweet taste).

Iris pseudacorus L.

IRIDACEAE

YELLOW FLAG Iris Family

OTHER NAMES *None*
HEIGHT *3'/9dm*
HABITAT *Swamps, wet ditches, lakesides*
SEASON *May–August*

Iris grows in crowded clumps in or near standing water or running streams, where it becomes an invasive plant much loved for its roots by muskrats and as cover by waterfowl. Emperor dragonfly larvae climb its smooth, straplike leaves to pupate and one can find their empty cases above the waterline. The iris's specific name comes from *pseudo*—false, and *Acorus calamus*—sweet flag, from the resemblance of the long narrow leaves to the latter species. Yellow flag is a European species at first cultivated and eventually naturalized in southern B.C. and in Manitoba where, though it is not common, there are also several bright blue species. Yellow flag is common in many parts of the United States.

Iris was sometimes called 'orris'. A powder is made from the rhizomes of an Italian species for its sweet violet scent. Orris powder forms the base of many violet perfumes, especially in talcum powder, toothpastes, and breath-sweeteners.

A wealth of history and legend attaches to this genus. Its generic name comes from the Greek Iris, messenger of the gods, and both the Greek and Latin words translate as 'a rainbow'—hence the coined word 'iridescent' or 'rainbow-bright'.

The iris can be traced to ancient Egypt (where it replaced the lotus as an art form), to Byzantium, Assyria, and Persia, where it represented the tree of life or divine triad. In early Christian times it became the symbol of the purity of baptism. The Chinese called it Tai-Ki and considered it the origin of all things, encompassing the dual principles of yin and yang.

Authentic records by Bishop (later Pope) Gregory refer to irises in connection with the barbarian conqueror of Gaul, Clovis, who was converted and crowned as the first Christian King of the Franks in AD 481. Legend, probably mixed with fact, has it that he was able to cross the Rhine at Frankfurt (the 'ford of the Franks') because he saw irises growing, proving that the river was shallow. Before the battle of Tolbiac in 496 Clovis dreamed that the golden toads emblazoned on his standard had been changed to lilies (or irises—flower names were interchangeable) by the Virgin Mary. Taking this as a good omen, he adopted the iris as his heraldic device.

Seven hundred years later Louis VII of France took the iris as the symbol for the Second Crusade, his standard being richly decorated with the Fleur-de-Louis, as it then became known. Eventually the name changed to fleur-de-lys and finally to fleur-de-lis as we now know it. Charles V of France reduced the number of iris symbols to three in 1376, to symbolize the Holy Trinity.

In Britain, fleurs-de-lis were included in King Edward III's coat of arms in 1340, in conformity with his claim to the French throne. These were also reduced to three sometime before 1411 when Henry IV's Great Seal showed the amended form. Succeeding monarchs retained the iris symbol throughout the centuries, but by the end of the eighteenth century, especially after the French Revolution, the claim of the kings of England to the throne of France became meaningless, and when a new form of the Royal Arms was designed to include the union of Great Britain and Ireland in 1801, the arms of the Kings of France were dropped. The fleur-de-lis is still, however, prominent on both the Imperial State Crown and St Edward's Crown, the latter used only at the Monarch's coronation. The symbol also appears on the Prince of Wales' coat of arms, but is not to be confused with his emblem of three ostrich plumes.

Before the end of the fifteenth century the fleur-de-lis was used to indicate North on mariners' cards. Shakespeare knew the iris as the flower-de-luce and refers to it several times, the most apt quotation here being from *Henry VI* Part I:

> Cropp'd are the flower-de-luces in your arms;
> Of England's coat one half is cut away.

In the twentieth century it is not only the well-known emblem of the Boy Scouts, but appears on the uniform of the Quebec Nordiques hockey team and on the helmets of the American football team known as the New Orleans Saints!

More than 500 years of recorded history—quite a story for a simple flower.

Mentzelia laevicaulis (Dougl.) T. & G. var. *parviflora* (Dougl.) C.L. Hitch.

LOASACEAE

BLAZING STAR Blazing Star Family

OTHER NAMES *None*
HEIGHT *6"–2'/15–60 cm*
HABITAT *Wasteland, roadsides, desert areas*
SEASON *June–August*

One could not wish for a better common name for this brilliant flower; the lemon yellow petals, sepals, and anywhere from ten to fifty stamens shine as though varnished against the rather scrawny, stiff-stemmed branches, which are sticky to touch and covered (look with your hand lens) with clusters of barbed hairs, as are the leaves. The outer stamens are wider at their base and look like narrow petals (petaloid); some are sterile (do not bear pollen).

The flower's perfect star, up to four inches across, opens in the heat of the day in arid regions. It grows in southern B.C. and valleys east of the Cascade Mountains as well as in the deserts of California, the coast ranges, southern Nevada, and east to Utah and Montana.

Of special interest is the prairie version of this flower, known as evening star or sand-lily (*M. decapetala*). It is creamy white and opens only in the evening. It grows on clay banks, eroded hillsides, and other wasteland and, although uncommon, is plentiful where established.

Blazing star is pollinated by bees and butterflies. As one would expect, evening star owes its survival to night-flying moths.

Both species make good biennial garden subjects if you live in a dry area, especially east of the Cascade Mountains. However, the thick, woody root must be dug carefully to avoid breaking it or the sparse feeding roots. (See inset.)

The generic name honors C. Mentzel, an early German botanist. The specific name means 'smooth-stemmed', and the varietal name means 'small'.

Mimulus alsinoides Dougl.

SCROPHULARIACEAE

LITTLE MONKEY-FLOWER Figwort Family

OTHER NAME *Chickweed Monkey-flower*
HEIGHT *1"–5"/2.5–13 cm*
HABITAT *Sheltered rock crevices; sunny, well-drained slopes*
SEASON *March–May*

This is the smallest of the several species of monkey-flower and is found in south-western B.C., the Cascade Mountains, and western Washington. In early spring the charming little laughing faces (*mimus*—a mimic) lift their bright gold to the sun, partially eclipsing the small grayish-green leaves. Each flower has a large crimson spot on the lower lip (smaller red spots may or may not be present), whereas *M. guttatus* (page 70) has many small ones.

The abbreviation Dougl. in the botanical name indicates that this was one of the large collection of new plants discovered and transported to England by David Douglas, who is briefly described on page 70.

The origin of the botanical family name is steeped in lore. Scrofula, a disease known in pre-Saxon times, was described in antique medical works as a skin lesion or a general painful swelling of the body, especially in the young. Today it is understood to be a constitutional malady affecting the lymphatic glands.

Decoctions and infusions of the roots and leaves of figwort plants were used, but the famous and dramatic remedy was to touch the person or clothing of the monarch, thereby miraculously removing The King's Evil (scrofula's other name). Edward the Confessor (canonized in 1161) wrought the first cure by touching a scrofulous person, and belief in the sovereign's healing power persisted until the death of Queen Anne in 1714.

Mimulus guttatus DC.

SCROPHULARIACEAE

COMMON MONKEY-FLOWER Figwort Family

OTHER NAMES *None*
HEIGHT *From semi-reclining to 20" / 50 cm*
HABITAT *Dripping cliff-faces, beside waterfalls, stream banks; sea level to moderate mountain elevations*
SEASON *May–September*

This brilliant flower is found in south-western B.C., southern Alberta and Saskatchewan, east and west Washington, and northern Oregon. There are eight more species in B.C., two more in Alberta, and one more in Saskatchewan. A very similar yellow-flowered species grows in Manitoba, as well as one with blue flowers. Monkey-flowers are easy to identify by shape alone, regardless of color. Compare the pink one on page 134 and the tiny yellow one on page 68.

M. *guttatus*, with the other two mentioned here and three others, was introduced to Britain from North America by David Douglas, a Scottish stonemason's son, born in 1799, who became one of the greatest exploring botanists of all time. His story makes fascinating reading and deserves mention here, however briefly.

Douglas travelled widely in western Canada and north-west America, discovering and collecting many species of plants, including the Douglas fir (named for him). To this day he is something of a folk hero to professional foresters in B.C., Oregon, and Washington. He was also a first-rate field naturalist and ornithologist. A man of immense energy, his interests encompassed the whole natural kingdom. His was not an age of intense specialization, but of variety in learning. Today it would take 40 scientists to collect, identify, and bring back as many new species from a vast, dangerous, unexplored country.

David Douglas died tragically at age thirty-five, trampled and gored by a trapped bull at the bottom of a wild cattle pit, during an exploration of one of the Sandwich Islands. Murder or suicide was quickly ruled out and it is assumed that being both extremely curious as well as near-sighted, he ventured too near the edge and fell in.

Nuphar polysepalum Engelm.

NYMPHAEACEAE

YELLOW WATER-LILY Water-Lily Family

OTHER NAMES *Yellow Pond Lily, Spatter-dock, Cow Lily*
HEIGHT *Water level*
HABITAT *Shallow lakes, slow streams, ponds*
SEASON *April–August*

Viewed from above, the flower is extremely interesting. The beautiful yellow that gives the flower its name consists entirely of sepals, not, as you might easily suppose, petals. There are usually four small cupped greenish sepals followed inwards by five much larger ones, greenish in bud, opening to a clear, pure yellow, turning red-orange as they die. The petals themselves number ten to eighteen and have become reduced to mere wedges that merge to form the extraordinary umbrella-shaped golden stigma in the center of the flower; it even has umbrella-like 'spokes' and is depressed in the center. The stamens at first crowd up the base of the stigma forming tiny 'scales' each outlined in red; as they mature they bend downwards and the anthers enlarge into dramatic crimson and purple structures that in turn become covered in pollen.

When the flower dies, the stigma, being pollinated, enlarges greatly and rises above water level as a very visible trumpet shape, glossy green, ridged and fluted, with a dirty yellow indented tip. The large floating leaves help to reduce overheating of shallow water in summer and provide docking facilities for small frogs and dragonflies, while beneath them fish feast on hosts of small aquatic life.

Nuphar derives from the Persian *nenuphar* (or *naufar*, according to some), a name for water-lily that has been taken unchanged into the French language. *Polysepalum* refers to the several sepals.

Water-lily seeds can be parched and eaten, but not the roots, contrary to many references to them in edible plant books.

Kwakiutl Indians call pond lily 'beaver's mat'. The Nootka call it 'west wind' because whenever the west wind blows the leaves stand up on the water. The roots were sliced, dried, and used as a decoction for asthma, chest pains, and heart disease by both Kwakiutl and Haida Indians. This is not a contradiction of the statement made above that the roots are inedible; it merely means that they should not be eaten as food; medicinal use of inedible plants is well known.

The species illustrated is found from Alaska through B.C. to northern California; eastward to western Alberta, Colorado, and South Dakota. A closely related yellow species (*N. variegatum*) is found from B.C. eastward to Newfoundland and southward to Montana, South Dakota, and Delaware. Other related yellow species are found in Saskatchewan and Manitoba.

Opuntia fragilis (Nutt.) Haw.

CACTACEAE

BRITTLE CACTUS Cactus Family

OTHER NAMES *Brittle Prickly Pear, Cholla*
HEIGHT *3"–4"/7.5–10 cm*
HABITAT *Desert regions, plains, and hills*
SEASON *June–July*

Desert, to many people, conjures up a vision of endless sand where nothing grows, of cloudless skies and scorching heat in some distant exotic land. Or it may mean the harsh deserts of Mexico or Arizona where cacti grow into immense branched 'candelabras'. It seems incongruous to imagine desert areas arid enough to support cacti in western Canada and the northern United States. Yet it is precisely here that this little cactus flourishes. Like its huge relatives in the south, it possesses means of conserving water, vital for its own survival and often for small animals, or people in distress, as the bitter juice can be tapped as a source of water.

Brittle cactus and starvation cactus (*O. polyacantha*) were eaten by B.C. Interior Indians, who scorched off the spines, of which there are up to nine in each pincushion. When squeezed, the inner flesh of a cooked segment popped out and was eaten either whole or used in cakes. The fruit is a fleshy berry about an inch long, which is used to make jelly or candy as well as being eaten cooked or raw. There are about 250 species of cacti, many well known as house plants, and all are edible.

Many cacti, including the one illustrated, have fragile, translucent petals and red, yellow-anthered stamens. Leaves have evolved into spines that do not transpire and the pads are coated with a layer of wax to prevent evaporation of stored water. Old pads or those with insufficient water grow wrinkled (see inset). Brittle cactus grows in large mats and the flowers create a lovely vision for a tired hiker, though the sharp spines can pierce any composition sole. By the time you have negotiated these when you are desperate for something to quench your thirst, you will have earned it!

Brittle cactus is abundant in B.C.'s dry interior, into the Rocky Mountains to about 6,000'/1,800 m, and across the southern prairie to eastern Manitoba. It grows on the drier islands of Puget Sound, and southwards to northern California and northern Arizona; and eastwards to northern Texas and southern Michigan.

Years ago members of the genus *Opuntia* were imported into Australia from California to be sold as house-plants. Unfortunately, many of them found their way outdoors where they flourished all too well because they had arrived 'clean' (without natural predators), and in time became a serious agricultural nuisance. Insects and fungi had to be imported to feed

on the cacti to retain a balance that nature had set up in the first place—in California!

Brittle cactus, as its name implies, can be broken easily, and individual segments will put down roots. These can be induced to grow at home and develop new segments *ad infinitum*; but getting them to bloom is quite another matter. The plants must have long hours of intense sunlight and heat, poor gravelly soil, and excellent drainage, or they will rot. Unless you live in a similar area, you might as well avoid disappointment by leaving the cacti in their own environment.

Potentilla fruticosa L.

ROSACEAE

SHRUBBY CINQUEFOIL Rose Family

OTHER NAMES *Yellow Rose, Five-Fingers, Buckbrush*
HEIGHT *1'–5'/3–15 dm*
HABITAT *Damp saline soil of plains and hills; tundra and dry plains;
      subalpine slopes and mountains to 9,000'/2,700 m*
SEASON *Late June – early August*

The shrubby cinquefoil is known to ranchers and wildlife biologists as an indicator plant. In overgrazed areas this plant, while not a preferred diet, may be eaten until it is stunted or killed, showing that there are more livestock than the range can accommodate.

The most usual form of growth for this attractive 'rose' is as a low, somewhat spreading shrub, and as such it is much prized in rock gardens. Being hardy, it is used to decorate public squares and other such places requiring flowers that do not need a great deal of care. Rooted branches may be cut, if any are found close to the ground; they will grow on almost unchecked if you give them gritty soil and very little food.

Shrubby cinquefoil is abundant across the western provinces, and in the Cypress Hills of Alberta and Saskatchewan it is in bloom until December. In Manitoba, Riding Mountain National Park includes an ideally windswept environment in the western meadows and grasslands where many wildflowers flourish, among them this cinquefoil.

Cinquefoil is an almost literal translation from the French 'five leaves'. *Potentilla* means powerful, as the plant was supposed to possess medicinal properties. *Fruticosa* means shrubby, and aptly describes the species.

Many other species of *Potentilla* can be recognized by five-petalled rose-like flowers and pale to brilliant yellow coloring. The leaves vary, but generally are green above and silvery gray beneath; not all are five-fingered.

In addition to the range mentioned above, shrubby cinquefoil is found from Alaska south through the Cascade Mountains and the Olympic Mountains to California, and through the Rocky Mountain States to Labrador, Nova Scotia, New Jersey, and Pennsylvania.

Potentilla pacifica Howell

ROSACEAE

PACIFIC SILVERWEED Rose Family

OTHER NAMES *Cinquefoil, Five-fingers*
HEIGHT *3″–18″/7.5–45 cm*
HABITAT *Marsh edges, beaches, sand dunes*
SEASON *June–September*

This flower has two English names that are also applied to the shrubby cinquefoil (*P. fruticosa*). The one under discussion is, as its name implies, found on the Pacific coast from Alaska to southern California. A very similar species grows in alkaline marshes throughout the prairie provinces and in the interior of B.C., as well as in the range mentioned above, though mostly east of the Cascade Mountains and east again to Atlanta, Georgia. It is named goosegrass (*P. anserina*) and the specific name means 'of geese'. Both species are interesting for their method of reproduction, which enables them to survive after heavily grazed *P. fruticosa* has been eliminated or stunted. Wherever a joint occurs on the stolons (supplementary stems running over the ground), roots are put down and leaves develop. As the parent plant dies these new shoots become individual plants. The plant is able to generate colonies rapidly and thus helps prevent overgrazing by deer and other animals. It is often found near waterholes when other plants have disappeared. *P. pacifica* and *P. anserina* transplant readily from a small piece of rooted stolon.

The roots are edible and taste something like parsnips or sweet potatoes. Indians steamed or roasted them.

The two yellow and one purple cinquefoils in this book are examples of similarity of species in a genus having common characteristics in leaves or flowers, although the growth is different. While you will not find growing every flower that has been illustrated here, or find here every flower you see, you can acquire a lot of understanding by comparing one member of a family or genus with another; cross-referencing here and there is to help you do this.

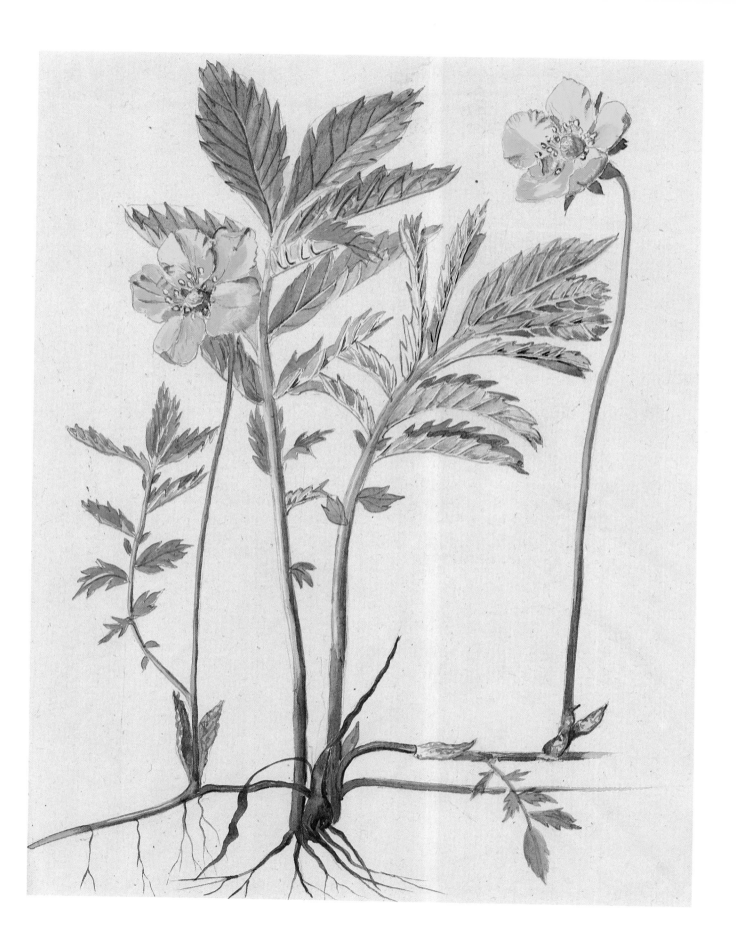

Ranunculus occidentalis Nutt.

RANUNCULACEAE

WESTERN BUTTERCUP Buttercup Family

OTHER NAME *Crowfoot*
HEIGHT *2"–20"/5–13 cm*
HABITAT *Moist, well-drained soil of grassy meadows; sunny rock slopes*
SEASON *April–May*

Is there anyone who has never seen a buttercup nor, as a child, held its glistening golden petals under a friend's chin to see 'if you love butter'? There are buttercups just about everywhere in Canada and the U.S.A. just as there are all over Europe. Some are pale yellow, others the well-known gold, and still others white or even slightly tinged with red. The list is endless. Thirteen species are listed for Saskatchewan and thirty for B.C., to mention only two vast areas. The species illustrated is the most common and widespread native western buttercup, as its specific name implies. The generic name is derived from the Latin *rana*—a frog, since many buttercups grow in soggy places inhabited by small frogs.

Western buttercup is found in profusion from Alaska to California, east through north-western Alberta, Saskatchewan, and Manitoba, and north-western U.S.A. There are many other species recognizable from the illustration of the western buttercup.

Buttercups contain irritants that blister the skin with prolonged contact. Haida Indians of B.C. used the fruits as a counter-irritant for boils and other skin infections.

Sedum spathulifolium Hook.

CRASSULACEAE

STONECROP Stonecrop Family

OTHER NAMES *Spatula-leaf Sedum, Broadleaf Sedum*
HEIGHT *6"–12"/15–30 cm*
HABITAT *Coastal cliffs, dry foothills, rocky outcrops*
SEASON *May–June*

Each leaf in the flat rosette of this attractive succulent is covered in a powdery 'bloom', like that on purple grapes, which rubs off directly when it is touched. Leaves and stem store enough moisture to sustain the plant over long periods of drought due to frozen soil and rapid run-off of surface water. The jewel-like colors in the leaves persist from flowering time to late fall.

This stonecrop grows on the Pacific coast from southern B.C. to California. Another species (*S. lanceolatum*) has short pointed leaves that are almost circular in cross-section (see insets) and similar but slightly darker flowers. It is found from Alaska and the Yukon to California, and east to Alberta, South Dakota, Nebraska, and Colorado, from sea level to subalpine areas. A very similar species (*S. stenopetalum*) grows from B.C. to California; in south-western Alberta and in the Cypress Hills of Alberta and Saskatchewan; and in the adjacent American states. Stonecrop is rare in Manitoba, being known only at The Pas, west of the northern end of Lake Winnipeg.

Sedum is from the Latin—a houseleek. The closely related genus *Sempervivum* (Latin *semper*—always, and *vivum*—alive) includes 'hens-and-chickens', well known in rock gardens. To establish the sedums mentioned here, cut a short piece of rooted stem and plant it directly in your garden, where it needs full sun, poor soil, and very little moisture. Sedums will grow but not bloom in semi-shade, and the leaves will remain gray-green all year.

Stonecrops are useful for the treatment of diarrhea and internal or external bleeding, either as an infusion or a poultice. Squirrels and deer relish the young leaves to the point where they need protection in the home garden.

Solidago canadensis L. var. *salebrosa* (Piper) Jones

COMPOSITAE

GOLDENROD Composite Family

OTHER NAMES *Graceful Goldenrod, Canada Goldenrod, Meadow Goldenrod*
HEIGHT *10″–12″/25–30 cm; 6′–7′/1.8–2.1 m; according to location.*
HABITAT *Gravelly roadsides, hedgerows, dampish ditches, meadow edges; rock outcrops; shores and clearings or open forest*
SEASON *June–September*

Goldenrod has an undeserved reputation for giving hay fever to people with pollen allergies. Studies have shown the pollen to be very heavy and not borne any distance by wind, so that unless you bury your nose in a spray of blossom, you should have no fear of entering goldenrod country in summer.

This is a transcontinental, ubiquitous plant. Short specimens grow in poor, dry places, tall ones in better soil. Such different habitats (see above) account for the wide range of height of this species. It is a striking flower at any height and one is usually granted a bonus in the form of dozens of crowding butterflies and other insects busily feeding and, of course, pollinating.

Goldenrod frequently grows close to purple asters and because they are color opposites, each makes the other appear brighter than it is by itself—a psychedelic effect that man can only create with certain clear pigments containing no black.

Old herbalists believed goldenrod to have curative properties (since disproved) and gave it the name *solidus*—whole, and *ago*—to make; and so . . . to cure.

Taraxacum officinale **Weber**

COMPOSITAE

DANDELION Composite Family

OTHER NAMES *Lion's Tooth, Blowball, Priest's Crown, Wet-a-Bed*
HEIGHT *4"–15"/10–37.5 cm*
HABITAT *Fields, lawns, roadsides, and waste places*
SEASON *April–August*

This is a prime example of a weed being no more than a plant that is unwelcome. Humble dandelion's golden flowers, 'lion-toothed' leaves, and long, succulent tap-root were cultivated before lawns and bowling-greens became fashionable and the plant came to be considered a noxious weed. It may be significant that dandelions are first mentioned in 1513. Henry VIII acceded to the throne in 1509 and in 1525 was given Hampton Court Palace by Cardinal Wolsey, where the King proceeded to create superb lawns and a bowling green (still there today). Lawns in those days were cut by hand with a scythe: imagine the consternation of an anxious gardener on seeing the first dandelion in His Majesty's velvet green (enough to have the poor man beheaded).

Dandelion has a great many uses. During World War II the ground-up roots were roasted and extensively used as a substitute in those coffee-less days. The plant is cultivated in France as a vegetable or salad; the growing leaves can be blanched for salads or picked and cooked when young—they are rich in vitamins A and C and minerals. The flowers are used to make wine and beer. Seedheads serve to augment the diet of many birds, especially finches and particularly pine siskins, which climb the waving stems to eat the seeds. Gypsies used to obtain a magenta dye from the roots, and Scotsmen made the same dye for their tartans from the whole plant or its roots. Experiments among weavers in North America have shown, however, that dandelions on this side of the Atlantic yield only a yellow dye.

The bitter milky juice that the whole plant exudes is said to cure warts if applied directly to them. Even more interesting is that in Russia another species (*T. koksaghyz*) forms an industrially usable latex heavily relied on during World War II as a source of rubber.

The specific name *officinale* is equivalent to early English 'medicinal', since dandelion leaves make a tea for coughs, fevers, and internal inflammations. The root is diuretic, hence one of the French names *pissenlit*— wet-a-bed. The other French name, *dent-de-lion*, and our dandelion, are from the Latin *dens*—tooth, and *leo*—lion, referring to the supposed resemblance of the deeply notched leaves to lions' teeth. *Taraxacum* appears to stem from the Greek *tarassein*—to stir up, presumably relating to the plant's medicinal properties.

More than a thousand kinds of dandelions have been listed; the one

illustrated is the common one with perfect ray florets throughout (having pistil and stamen); the flower stems are smooth and hollow, growing from the center of the flat rosette of leaves (they may be more upright in shady locations with better soil than is their usual habitat).

I am often surprised and delighted by the hardy wildflowers that brighten a dreary sidewalk or the base of a factory wall. Foremost is the dandelion pushing its tiny seedling through minute cracks in the concrete to form its rosette of leaves and brilliant flowers, no matter how dwarfed by poor conditions.

Viola glabella Nutt.

VIOLACEAE

YELLOW VIOLET Violet Family

OTHER NAMES *Stream Violet, Smooth Violet, Pioneer Violet*
HEIGHT *9"–12"/23–30 cm*
HABITAT *Light shade of moist banks and open woods; stream edges*
SEASON *April–May*

The novice may well ask how this flower can be called a violet when it is bright yellow. The answer lies in the family and genus names (for which, incidentally, the proper accentuation is *vi*olaceae and *vi*ola), since the physical characteristics of the plant place it in this family, regardless of color. *Glabella* means smooth, referring to the hairless leaves of this rather tall member of the genus. The flowers have no perfume. The leaves are usually heart-shaped with serrated edges, pointed, with petioles up to three times longer than the leaf blades.

The nectary is a backward prolongation of the lower petal into a hollow 'spur' into which honeybees (in violets with short spurs) and butterflies with long probosces (in long-spurred species) are led by purple honey-guides when they land on the lower petal. Insects carrying pollen from another flower in the species bump the pollen-carrying anthers in probing for nectar. At the same time, hairs (beards) on the side petals and style comb the pollen collected on their bodies from the previous flower. The arrangement of the vital parts of violets is such that self-fertilization is virtually impossible, but is favorable to cross-pollination. This violet is instantly attractive to bees sensitive to yellow; violets of other colors have some yellow in their throats, as do blue irises, for instance.

There are several yellow violets: this one grows in B.C., Alberta, and Alaska, and south to California. Yellow prairie violet (*V. nuttallii*) and 'Saskatchewan' violet (*V. vallicola*) grow in Alberta, Saskatchewan, Washington, and Oregon. Southern Manitoba and the adjacent United States have two: the downy yellow (*V. pubescens*) and yellow wood violet (*V. pensylvanica*).

There are numbers of violets other than yellow, most having showy blue, violet, or white flowers; thirty-three species (including yellow) are listed for the Pacific Northwest. Those flowers that are not showy enough to warrant cultivation are often cleistogamous, that is to say, seeds are set without the flower ever opening, as it does not require a pollinator. Those that do, have attractive seed pods that open into three narrow boat-shaped containers for a row of minute smooth, round black seeds (see enlarged inset). Some violets have long leaves, some are hairy, some smooth. They transplant readily to the home garden and may even become a bit invasive: the species illustrated here will make a large clump that may need dividing; once established in fairly moist semi-shade it will propagate from self-sown seeds.

Aquilegia formosa Fisch.

RANUNCULACEAE

WESTERN COLUMBINE Buttercup Family

OTHER NAME *Red Columbine*
HEIGHT *24″–30″/60–75 cm on plains; 8″–24″/20–60 cm at higher elevations*
HABITAT *Rockslides and outcrops; shady aspen groves and ravines; mountains to 11,000′/3,000 m; roadside hedges; edges of coniferous forest*
SEASON *May–August*

In the Uffizi Gallery in Florence there is an altar-piece by a fifteenth-century painter in which part of the detail shows a simple tumbler containing a few pinks and a single stem of deep blue columbines. They are so rich, so vibrant with life after nearly 500 years, that you feel the leaves will begin to stir or a petal may drop softly. People have delighted in this wildflower for a long, long time.

Western columbine is found from Alaska through B.C. and south to California, and in western Alberta, Utah, and Montana. It is so similar in form to other columbines that the whole genus can be recognized easily. The plant has a dainty, open growth so that each thin leaf may receive maximum light. The unique shape of the drooping flower with its five red-orange sepals and tubular petals, which form nectaries deep enough that only long-tongued insects and hummingbirds pollinate them, reminds one of the gay cap-and-bells of medieval court jesters.

A blue columbine (*A. brevistyla*) grows in Alaska and B.C.'s northern Rockies, and in Alberta's forest and in northern and eastern Saskatchewan and Manitoba, as well as in South Dakota. *A. flavescens* is a yellow alpine species, often tinged with pink or scarlet, found in the Cascade Mountains, and from B.C. to Washington, Alberta, Idaho, Montana, Colorado, and Utah.

The generic name is from *aquila*, an eagle, the spurs being likened to talons. *Formosa* means 'beautiful', and 'columbine' comes from *columba*, a dove.

Ripe seeds started in flats and transplanted to semi-shade should flourish in the home garden, where in time they will self-seed. They hybridize easily with other columbines, which may produce interesting forms and colors.

Lilium columbianum Hanson

LILIACEAE

TIGER LILY Lily Family

OTHER NAMES *Columbia Lily, Turk's Cap, Oregon Lily*
HEIGHT *2'–5'/3–15 dm*
HABITAT *Damp woods, open meadows, roadside hedges*
SEASON *June–July; August in mountains 3,000'–4,000'/900–1,200 m*

This spectacular lily is found in the moist interior, on the coast, and (sparsely) in the dry Columbia Valley in B.C., south-east to Idaho, and south to northern California. It seems odd that it should be less common in the place from which the flower takes its name: however, the first specimen named came from Oregon, possibly from along the Columbia River.

In good soil the plant may bear as many as thirty-two blooms, any of which may reach four-and-a-half inches across. As the aging flower recurves its tepals the common name of Turk's cap becomes obviously apt. Less obvious is the derivation alluding to a special form of turban adopted by Sultan Muhammed I, called a martagon, and there is a Turk's cap lily botanically designated as *L. martagon*.

The lily goes through several color changes as the pale bud opens and the tepals become deeper orange. The anthers dangle from delicate green filaments and change from deep red to cinnamon brown. In the young flower the filaments and anthers are straight; as they mature the anthers curve outwards, dangling loosely at the tips of their filaments, which facilitates the dropping of pollen onto an insect searching for nectar secreted in grooves at the base of the petals. At this stage the long angled pistil is visible.

Tiger lily bulbs were eaten by many Indian peoples in meat stews, although the taste is bitter. Today it is not a good thing to dig up a wild lily, unless it is threatened by bulldozers. One can attempt rescue by digging deep (12″/30 cm or more—the bigger the plant, the deeper the bulb), ideally when the leaves have died down. Individual bulb scales can be grown in pots.

Lonicera ciliosa (Pursh) DC.

CAPRIFOLIACEAE

ORANGE HONEYSUCKLE Honeysuckle Family

OTHER NAMES *Trumpet, Northwest Honeysuckle*
HEIGHT *Climbing to 20′/6 m or more*
HABITAT *Coniferous forests, mixed woods, hedgerows*
SEASON *May–June*

Many a sapling fir or maple bears the scars of the stranglehold sometimes exerted by this woody vine that all but kills the victims. The stems may be half an inch thick, covered with stringy bark, whose twisted strands drape themselves from trees in ropelike masses. In its effort to reach the light, honeysuckle climbs high and in its course illumines forest or hedgerow with brilliant orange trumpet-shaped flowers that do not, unfortunately, possess the perfume of English honeysuckle. Hummingbirds and swallow-tail butterflies, attracted to them by color, are able to reach the nectar with their long tongues and probosces respectively. Compare with another flower with a long nectary, the columbine on page 90.

In late summer the pale green fruit ripen into bright red, translucent berries within the pair of cup-shaped leaves (visible as a green cluster in the illustration). The berries are reputed to be poisonous and are best left alone; even animals seem to give them a wide berth.

Of the many species of honeysuckle, the one illustrated is found in B.C., and from California to Arizona to Montana. Several are found in the Prairie provinces, usually yellow turning to orange-red with age. All have the characteristic tubular flower.

A sixteenth-century German herbalist, Adam Lonitzer, is honored by the generic name. *Ciliosa* means 'hairy' or 'ciliate' because the flower tube is densely hairy inside and, although the leaves are smooth, their margins are covered with very fine hairs.

 *RED*

Gilia aggregata (Pursh) Spreng.

POLEMONIACEAE

SCARLET GILIA Phlox Family

OTHER NAMES *Sky Rocket, Foxfire, Polecat Plant*
HEIGHT *4″–3′ / 1–9 dm*
HABITAT *Dry prairie, subalpine broken rock areas; open woods, meadows, hills*
SEASON *May–August*

Sheer barbarity of color is offset by daintiness of form—a long slender corolla tube slightly flared into five symmetrical, white-spotted, satin-textured, pointed petals, and rather drab leaves. The name of a Spanish botanist, Felipe Luis Gil, is perpetuated in the genus *Gilia*, subtly reminding us of that land of dramatic emotions and sun-drenched, violent color contrasts. *Aggregata* means clustered, referring to the flowers.

While scarlet is the most common form, there are gilias with yellow or white flowers. The scarlet is found in ponderosa pine-sagebrush country in southern B.C. and in adjacent land in the United States, and also in the Sierra Nevadas and northern Coast Range. The flowers wilt immediately they are picked and will not revive. You might raise a few seeds (the flower produces but few, maybe only one or two). You probably stand a better chance of success if you live east of the Cascade Mountains. Transplant the young gilias to a sunny site where they may increase voluntarily from shed seeds.

Some authorities refer to this genus as *Ipomopsis*, but there is no obvious difference in the two genera.

Okanagan Indians prize the leaves for their tonic properties. Steeped until hot water turns bright green, the leaves are removed and the medicine taken in small doses. This contradicts a report that the plant is poisonous, as does the fact that sheep graze it without ill effect. But then many a poisonous herb yields valuable medication if it is correctly prepared and administered. In general it is as well to exercise caution and leave the plant alone.

Rumex acetosella L.

POLYGONACEAE

SHEEP SORREL Buckwheat Family

OTHER NAMES *Common Sorrel, Sour Grass, Sheep-, Red-, Cow-,*
Mountain-, Field-, or Horse Sorrel
HEIGHT *6"–2'/15–60 dm*
HABITAT *Dry soil in rock crevices, dry woodlands*
SEASON *May–August*

This well-known garden weed invades rockeries with alarming speed by means of hair-like running root-stocks. The minute flowers when seen in a group give a misty red effect, but some are insignificant and yellow, depending on the amount of sun that reaches the plant. It is related to dock, another noxious weed, and both produce quantities of tiny seeds. But of course, weeds are only 'noxious' to humans. Sheep sorrel and its relatives are important to wildlife: ground-feeding birds eat the seeds, as do marsh and shorebirds; herbivorous animals such as the cottontail and deer eat the leaves; some mice and squirrels eat both seeds and leaves. So do we, for that matter, in salads or made into green soup in the French manner.

The plant is an indicator of acid soil, and its flavor is distinctly acid, hence its name: Latin *rumex*—sorrel, and *acetum*—acid. The leaves contain oxalic acid (as do rhubarb leaves, in sufficient concentration to make them poisonous).

The species illustrated is introduced and has become naturalized over most of Canada and the United States.

Medicinally, this and a larger species of sorrel are refrigerant and diuretic; the juice applied as a paste in a mixture of burnt alum and citric acid is used for skin tumors.

PINK

Allium cernuum **Roth.**

LILIACEAE

NODDING ONION Lily Family

OTHER NAMES *Wild Onion, Wild Garlic, Leek, Chives*
HEIGHT *5"–20"/13–50 cm*
HABITAT *Rocky or gravelly soil, parkland prairies, thickets and open slopes*
SEASON *June–August*

The flower closely resembles garden chives and is much relished by native Indians who 'barbecue' the strong-tasting bulb in underground steaming pits, either alone or for flavoring other food, such as black tree lichen.

Although the plant tastes of onion rather than garlic, one of its names is still apt, since *allium* is the Latin for garlic. The specific name means 'having the face towards the ground' from the graceful downward curve of the flower stem.

There are many species of wild onion, most having white-to-pink flowers with three true petals and three similar sepals. These are known collectively as 'tepals', having the same form and color. Another flower with very distinctive tepals is the calypso or false ladyslipper (page 114).

Nodding onion is found throughout Canada, and south into Washington and Oregon, central Idaho, west Montana, and to Mexico and Georgia.

Antennaria microphylla Rydb.
COMPOSITAE

ROSY PUSSYTOES Composite Family

OTHER NAMES *Cat's-paws, Everlasting, Ladies-tobacco*
HEIGHT *2″–12″/5–30 cm*
HABITAT *Sandy well-drained, rather rocky terrain; plains and valleys;
 mountains to 9,000′/2,700 m*
SEASON *Late May–early August according to elevation*

This little 'everlasting' is sometimes confused with pearly everlasting (*Anaphalis*); it is not only much smaller than the 'pearly', which rises to 3′/9 dm, but is usually pink where the other is white. Pistils and stamens are on different plants. Mats of rosy pussytoes cover areas several feet wide and in the early stages of blooming the flower-heads nod; later they straighten up.

Although tiny, pussytoes is very decorative. The papery bracts remain on the plant indefinitely and a few flowers cut and hung to dry will last throughout the winter—hence one of the common names. *Antennaria* derives from the supposed resemblance to the antennae of insects, and *micro*—small, *phyllum*—leaf, form the specific name. At high altitudes the flowers bloom on short stems and are likely to be more brilliantly pink. Leaves on the taller plants are apt to be longer and narrower. Most of the many western *Antennaria* species have whitish or faintly pink flowers: the one illustrated is easily the most vivid. It is found from B.C. to Manitoba and from Washington to California.

This modest little plant has had quite a chequered career. Since its discovery in 1881 it has had its name changed more than once, and as it is considered by some authorities to be synonymous in botanical nomenclature with two other species—which will never do—it may undergo yet another name-change. Botanists must constantly strive for greater accuracy in their descriptions as more species are discovered. Rosy pussytoes used to be known as *A. rosea*, which you will still find in wildflower books published before 1973.

The insets show: top right—enlarged flower and a single pink bract; bottom left—front and back view of enlarged leaf.

Apocynum androsaemifolium L.

APOCYNACEAE

SPREADING DOGBANE Dogbane Family

OTHER NAMES *Flytrap Dogbane, Bitter-root*
HEIGHT *8"–24"/2–6 dm in B.C.; 1'–4'/3–12 dm on prairie*
HABITAT *Woodlands and light sandy soil; dry roadsides*
SEASON *June–September*

Massed together in full sun along a dry roadside, dogbane's small pink flowers set against dark green leaves are fairly showy, but one needs to look more closely to discover the bloom's individual charm and sweet perfume. The scent attracts many insects throughout the long blooming season and honey from this plant is much relished. But the blossom is also a deadly trap for some of the smaller insects. Strong pollinators like bumblebees or large butterflies with long proboscs can withdraw in time from the curiously constructed nectaries, which have inverted V-shaped openings within the dainty bell of the flower; but weak insects become caught by their mouths and cannot escape. Dead flies and small moths can be seen adhering to many flowers in any patch of dogbane. The pronged dark red claw-like seed pods (follicles) appear in August while the plant is still in bloom.

The name comes from the Greek *apo*—against, and *kyon*—a dog, but the original reason for the name is lost today.

When the stem—or even one of the small drooping leaves—is broken, a bitter white juice appears. This is a form of latex that could be made into rubber if quantities justified collection. The juice is toxic and browsing animals avoid the plant.

Spreading dogbane and a close relative, Indian hemp (*A. cannabinum*), were important to native tribes as a source of fiber from which they made fishing lines and nets.

Spreading dogbane is common across Canada and has been reported as far north as 165 miles south of Churchill, Manitoba. It extends across all but the south-eastern states of the U.S.A.

Asclepias speciosa Torr.

ASCLEPIADACEAE

SHOWY MILKWEED Milkweed Family

OTHER NAMES *Silkweed, Butterflyweed, Common Milkweed, Greek*
Milkweed
HEIGHT *2'–4'/6–12 dm*
HABITAT *Loamy to sandy soil, along waterways*
SEASON *May–July*

The first thing you notice about milkweed is its heavy, exotic perfume, which is said to induce drowsiness and might once have been distilled into a sleeping potion. That intriguing thought, added to the plant's unique relationship with the famous Monarch butterfly (about which more later) lends to this plant a mysterious quality that makes it exceptionally interesting.

The flowers are worth close examination. For one thing, the petals are not where you think they are. Below the curious pink, pointed hoods with their little horns that curve out from the base of each to touch the central green pistil, are five reddish petals that curve backwards towards the stem. Between these are five sepals (see inset).

When the flowers have been pollinated, the beautiful seed pods form singly or in groups of two or three, occasionally five, on steeply curved stems. At first they are woolly, with soft little spines sticking out all over, but in time the pod hardens and then splits along one side to reveal tightly packed seeds, each closely overlapping the next like brown scales. Attached to each seed is the still folded 'parachute' of soft white filaments, which look and feel like silk (they were in fact used by early settlers to fill pillows and bed covers and were considered warmer than feathers).

When the seeds ripen, the pods open wide and there appears a marvellous effervescence of brilliant silk foaming from each pod, seeds clinging to the placenta by a few silken filaments until a puff of wind carries them away to be deposited somewhere, one hopes to fulfil their destiny. The departure stage is illustrated. Note also the enlarged seed (achene) and the diagrammatic flower seen from above and from the side.

There is no resemblance or relationship between milkweed and orchids but their intricate methods of pollination are identical. In the case of milkweed its most intimate insect associate is the beautiful Monarch butterfly (*Danaus plexippus*), which in September migrates from southern Canada to areas extending from California to Florida and Mexico, where it spends the winter half asleep, usually on trees, which the lovely creatures adorn like strange flowers.

The strong perfume of milkweed, coupled with the sticky latex the plant exudes if punctured, tends to make insects drowsy, and some avoid

the plant altogether. The Monarch is a notable exception and it has developed a peculiar affinity for milkweed, upon whose leaves it lays its eggs. The larvae hatch and feed on the plant, absorbing from it the bitter, poisonous sap, which remains in their systems through pupation to maturity and for the rest of their lives, making them unpalatable to birds and therefore immune to predation. The Monarch's striking black and white spots on an orange-brown ground would seem to have come by association to trigger the birds' aversion, possibly on the 'once-bitten-twice-shy' principle, rather than by instinct. Even more remarkable is that birds also give the tasty Viceroy butterflies a wide berth, presumably because they have evolved similar coloring to the Monarch as a protective device.

Proof of the Monarch–milkweed interdependence was established in the 1840s when some milkweed was introduced to the isolated Sandwich Islands (Captain Cook's name for the Hawaiian Islands) and three years later Monarch butterflies appeared and bred, never having been seen before in that part of the world.

There are about 250 genera and 2,000 species of milkweed and all contain tough fibres like those found in flax, from which strong string can be twisted by hand. The plant illustrated has been used for centuries as food and medicine (it is necessary to be sure of identification). Young leaves or shoots can be covered in boiling water and cooked, using several changes of water to remove any bitterness: the taste is a little like asparagus. Young pods cooked in this manner are pleasant, the seeds becoming a soft mass. Just remember two things: the seeds become poisonous with age, and milkweed must never be eaten raw. Native Indian peoples still use the plant for treating warts, ringworm, and various abrasions and infections.

The plant's latex referred to earlier dries like soft rubber and can be used as such in emergencies; and after the living milkweed has given its all to the butterflies, humans, and others, the dying plant still has a gift to offer: when all the seeds have gone the hard open pods make attractive house decorations.

The name Asclepias comes from Asklepios, the Greek god of medicine, better known by his Latin name Aesculapius, a son of Apollo, who was raised by the centaur Chiron. Legend has it that Aesculapius acquired from Chiron such a wealth of knowledge of medicinal herbs that he restored the dead to life. His insignia was a staff entwined by a snake, and this remains the symbol of healing to this day.

Milkweed can be grown from seed or a piece of creeping rootstock. It takes about two years to bloom from the latter, and seedlings, of course, take longer. The plant is somewhat invasive, but butterflies and hummingbirds are attracted to it and you can always hope that you might inveigle a gorgeous Monarch to your garden.

Showy milkweed is to be found from coast to coast in Canada, south to California, east of the Cascade Mountains, and in the central United States.

Calypso bulbosa (L.) Oakes

ORCHIDACEAE

CALYPSO Orchid Family

OTHER NAMES *Venus' Slipper, Lady's Slipper, False Lady's Slipper,*
Deer-head Orchid, Cythera, Hider-of-the-North
HEIGHT *4"–7"/10–18 cm*
HABITAT *Cool, moist coniferous woods, damp spruce-aspen forests;*
mossy woods
SEASON *B.C. late April – July according to elevation; western and*
northern Alberta Hills, late May – early June; southern
Saskatchewan, Manitoba, May–June; California–Alaska,
May–July; also Colorado and Arizona

The tepals—three sepals and two petals alike in color and form—stand erect like plumes on the helmet of a medieval knight when the subtly scented flower is young, but as it ages, or when it is raining, they droop over the sac opening. A shapely pink hood also protects the reproductive organs and pollen within. The flower color changes with age from orchid pink to pale yellow, finally white, making some people think it is a different orchid species.

In April, when woodland mosses are damp and green, Calypso raises her pinky-mauve stem, along which grow several sheath-like bracts. Growing from the same corm is a single bright green leaf that becomes ridged and tinged with purple as it matures. When the flower has been pollinated, it dies, as does the leaf, and for a time the plant is no longer visible. The leaf is replaced in the fall by another, which persists through the winter.

Calypso was a mythical goddess, daughter of Atlas and seductress of Homer's Ulysses, when he was wrecked on her island of Ogyia. Her Greek name means concealment; this orchid is mainly found in deeply shaded places, half-hidden by mosses, grasses, and forest debris. The specific name simply means bulbous.

This exquisite flower is disappearing at an ever-accelerating pace due to urban encroachment on its habitat, and picking. An additional and unusual cause of its decline is the little-known fact that when it was plentiful the corm was in great demand by herbalists in China. Untold thousands of plants were dug up by Chinese immigrants and sent to their homeland. It is related that the diggers could never get enough corms to supply the market. The practice has perforce ceased as there are no longer sufficient quantities to warrant harvesting.

Please resist the temptation to pick the flower or transplant the corm. Its thread-like roots will be damaged by the slightest movement. Furthermore, this species grows *in association with certain types of soil fungi* and cannot survive away from its natural habitat, no matter how much soil you take with you, because it must be constantly renewed in its natural state.

Chimaphila umbellata (L.) Bart. var. *occidentalis* (Rydb.) Blake

ERICACEAE

PRINCE'S PINE Heath Family

OTHER NAMES *Pipsissewa, Wintergreen, Waxflower, Ground Holly, Western Prince's Pine*
HEIGHT *4"–12"/10–30 cm*
HABITAT *Coniferous forest, beside mountain streams, in wet or dry soil from sea level to 8,000'/2,400 m*
SEASON *June–August*

This charming denizen of the forest is evergreen, as one of its names implies (Greek *cheima*—winter, and *philos*—loving). Its unusual leaves are wider at the tip than at the base and are wax-glossed and saw-toothed. No other leaves on the forest floor look like them. Note the curious stamens, which radiate as from a wheel around the fat red or green ovary. The flower, which may be pink or cream-colored, has a slight perfume and is pollinated by small flies.

Pipsissewa once had a considerable medicinal reputation among whites and Indians. The leaves contain ericolin and tannin, and were used in infusions for bladder stones. The plant is still used in parts of Central Europe as a home remedy for wounds. In at least one modern book on plant drugs it is given a place as an astringent and tonic and as a remedy for rheumatic and kidney afflictions.

Cree Indians called the plant 'pipisisikweu'; they and the early pioneers used the leaves as a tea substitute either alone or with labrador-tea (page 34).

Distribution is from Alaska through B.C. to southern California, east to the mountains of Colorado, to Georgia, Ohio, Illinois, and Utah.

Dodecatheon hendersonii Gray

PRIMULACEAE

BROAD-LEAVED SHOOTING STAR Primrose Family

OTHER NAME *Peacock*
HEIGHT *6"–12"/15–30 cm, occasionally 24"/60 cm*
HABITAT *Rocky bluffs and shallow-soil meadows with abundant spring*
        moisture but dry in summer. Coastal flats to mountain
        meadows above timber line
SEASON *Mid-April – early June*

Notice the breadth of the smooth, untoothed leaves pressed against the ground in a rosette and how they taper abruptly at the petiole (leaf-stalk). The flowers atop their smooth, straight stem seem to be astonished to have grown so tall: the surprised-looking, backward-curving petals may vary from flower to flower from palest pink to light orchid, rose-purple, or deep purple, with an occasional white flower, and all in the space of a few yards. The close-gathered bundle of down-pointing stamens and stigma look black but are purple. The 'dodie', as it is affectionately known, grows tall if the soil is deep and rich, and may have fifteen or twenty blooms to a stem. The single flower inset is enlarged about three times to show the details.

This 'dodie' grows on Vancouver and the Gulf Islands (but not the Queen Charlottes), south to southern Oregon, and is widespread in California, Idaho, and Montana.

There are several species of shooting star in the western provinces, one of them being white (*D. dentatum*) with untypical, toothed leaves; other species usually have long rather than rounded leaves, but all are easily recognizable from the illustration, which is typical.

The resounding generic name comes from the Greek *dodeka*—twelve, and *theoi*—gods.

Shooting star has various fanciful names in Indian languages, such as rain's navel (Haida), curlew's bill (Okanagan), and beautiful maiden (Thompson).

Epilobium angustifolium L.

ONAGRACEAE

FIREWEED Evening Primrose Family

OTHER NAMES *Willow-herb, Blooming Sally*
HEIGHT *Average 30"/75 cm but may reach 6'–9'/18–27 dm*
HABITAT *Wasteland, particularly burned areas*
SEASON *June–September*

Drastic changes in soil conditions, caused by the denuding of forest trees by fire, for instance, or the bombing of a city such as London during World War II, stimulate growth of the aptly named fireweed, which may cover acres or miles in a sea of magenta blossom, to the comfort of many small and not-so-small creatures seeking cover and food amid the general devastation. Nature's hurry to cover nakedness is nowhere more apparent. It will take years for the trees to grow from seed, but in the meantime, light reaching the ground encourages rapid growth of new small plants such as wild strawberry, bunchberry, heart-leaved arnica, and fireweed, among others. These fresh carpets of beauty stabilize soil that would otherwise blow away or be washed out by rains. As years pass, the carboned trunks add charcoal and humus to the soil as they disintegrate, and in about 200 years a new forest will mature.

Fireweed's seeds are contained in long slender ovaries that split and curl back when their contents are ripe. At this point they may in good conscience be brought home to give unusual character to dried grass arrangements. The flower is the official emblem of the Yukon.

Fireweed is transcontinental in its range. Indians used to use the tough fiber in the stems for twine and fishnets, and modern Indians still prize the young leaves and new shoots as edible greens, and also eat the sweet, glutinous pith in the stems.

Fireweed's name has its roots in Greek and Latin: Greek *epi*—upon, and *lobos*—pod, referring to the inferior ovary. The specific name derives from Latin *angustus*—narrow, and *folium*—leaf.

Geranium viscosissimum F. & M.

GERANIACEAE

STICKY GERANIUM Geranium Family

OTHER NAMES *Pink Geranium, Crane's-bill*
HEIGHT *10"–30"/25–75 cm*
HABITAT *Open woods, creek banks, roadsides, and meadows*
SEASON *May–July*

Viscosissimum means very sticky or viscous and this attractive, shrubby-looking plant is well named; it will adhere to your fingers and clothing, leaving a distinctly sticky deposit. This comes from the fine, gummy hairs that protect the whole plant from pollen-theft by ants and other unwanted crawling insects. Flower color in this genus may vary from bright pink to deep purple in B.C., Alberta, and Saskatchewan, and in Manitoba *G. bicknellii* has small, pink flowers; there is also a white species (*G. carolinianum*).

In the United States distribution of the three species is as follows:

G. viscosissimum: east Washington, Oregon, the Columbia River gorge, northern California, and Nevada.

G. bicknellii: western Washington and Oregon to northern Coast Ranges of California, and the Rocky Mountains and Utah.

G. carolinianum: throughout the Pacific Northwest and across most of the country.

Geranium leaves look like those of the larkspurs (page 168) but are distinguished by gland-tipped hairs. Garden and window-box geraniums belong to the same family but to a different genus (*Pelargonium*).

Sticky geranium is valuable as a forage plant for elk and deer in spring and summer. Bears eat the whole plant while moose prefer the flowers and upper leaves to most other vegetation.

Geranium comes from the Greek *geranos*—crane, referring to the long-beaked fruit, giving rise to one of its English names, crane's-bill.

Geum triflorum Pursh

ROSACEAE

THREE-FLOWERED AVENS Rose Family

OTHER NAMES *Prairie Smoke, Long-plumed Avens, Old Man's Whiskers, Torch Flower*
HEIGHT *3"–12"/7.5–30 cm*
HABITAT *Moister parts of sagebrush country, to lower mountain ridges*
SEASON *May – early July*

The deeply cut leaves of this plant are among the first green things to appear as the snow recedes. As the weather warms, the dainty triple flowers appear (*tri*—three, and *florum*—flowers), each with pink petals enclosed in a pink calyx and equally pink bracts that are longer than the petals. After pollination the faded flowers are replaced by elegant fluffy heads of pink and silver and green plumes, each with its brown seed attached to the receptacle, from which it is blown by the wind to start a new colony of plants.

The avens illustrated, together with several other purple or yellow-flowered species, grows in the dry interior of B.C., mostly east of the Cascade Mountains, and in the Cypress Hills area of Alberta and Saskatchewan. In Manitoba *G. triflorum* is found in the western section of Riding Mountain National Park and on prairie and clearings in the southern portion of the province. In the U.S.A. it continues south to California, mostly east of the Cascade Mountains, and can be found in several eastern states, including New York.

The large, bright pink rhizome was used by the Thompson Indians both as a tea and, in stronger doses, as a tonic. A brew was made for use in the sweat-house as a body wash for aches and pains. Ripe seeds were crushed and used as perfume: its use as a medicinal plant was versatile. The genus was known in ancient Greece: *geuo*—agreeable fragrance, or *genein*—to taste. Geum is also the old Latin name for a species known in England as herb-bennet.

The insets show, from top to bottom: a single achene, a seedhead, cross-section of root.

Kalmia polifolia Wang.

ERICACEAE

SWAMP LAUREL Heath Family

OTHER NAMES *Mountain Laurel, Pale Laurel, American Laurel, Bog Laurel*
HEIGHT *2′–3′/6–9 dm*
HABITAT *Cold, acid bogs*
SEASON *May–September*

Gently touch a stamen with a blade of grass and watch closely: you may be quick enough to see it whip upwards from its neat socket. The anther, when anchored like this, is still unripe and therefore not ready to release pollen through the tiny apertures created for the purpose, and this startling response may be to prevent self-fertilization of the receptive stigma. Instead, insects visiting other ripe-anthered flowers in the species effectively cross-pollinate.

Swamp laurel is related to the garden rhododendron. It grows from B.C. through Manitoba and eastward; south to California and east to Idaho in the U.S.A. The sculptured beauty of the buds and the extraordinary mechanism of the flowers deserve a close look with a hand lens. Swamp laurel is poisonous to cattle and sheep, and honey from it is said to be toxic.

The name *Kalmia* was given for Peter Kalm, a student of Linnaeus. *Polifolia* comes from Latin *polio*—to whiten, and *folium*—a leaf, referring to the gray or whitish undersurface of the leaves. The plant was first collected by a renowned naturalist, Sir Joseph Banks (1743–1820), in Newfoundland, and specimens were sent by sea to Kew Gardens. Few survived the disastrous storm that overtook the vessel, but these flourished and were greatly admired. We owe a great deal to botanists through the centuries who undertook perilous voyages and endured unimaginable hardships in their quests for plant knowledge, some dying from exposure or disease in times when there was no medical help available.

 *Lathyrus latifolius* L.

LEGUMINOSEAE

PERENNIAL PEA Pea Family

OTHER NAME *Everlasting Pea*
HEIGHT *Trailing, climbing 6'–8' / 18–24 dm*
HABITAT *Railway cuttings, roadsides, clay banks by the sea*
SEASON *July–September*

About ten species of wild peas grow in the Pacific Northwest, these being essentially coastal plants, most of which range in color from white to pink. All have the typical form of garden sweet peas, with a butterfly-wing 'standard' (the old generic name was *papillionaceae*—butterfly); below the standard is the 'wing', below which is the 'keel'. Wild peas are not scented.

The pea illustrated has flowers almost as large as the garden varieties and is by far the showiest of the wild peas with its raceme of blooms at the top of a ridged, gray-green stem. The leaves are interesting: each leaf consists of a leafstalk with flattened ridges, a pair of pointed oval leaflets with four or five long coiling tendrils at the tip, and a pair of broad appendages (stipules) at the base that clasp the bottom of the leaf-stalk and the stem. The vine entwines itself by means of its tendrils, climbing through hedgerows until they appear bright pink with pea blossoms; on the hard dry soil of coastal banks perennial pea trails along the ground. The plant is a naturalized garden escape.

Other species to look for from Vancouver Island to California are *L. littoralis*, a beach pea as its name implies, and *L. nevadensis*, which extends to Nevada. Alberta has *L. venosus* var. *intonsus*, common in wooded areas in July, and *L. ochroleucus*, which is yellowish-white as described in the specific name. All the others are various shades of pink or purple-pink.

 *Lewisia rediviva* **Pursh**

PORTULACACEAE

BITTER-ROOT Purslane Family

OTHER NAMES *Spatlum, Desert Rose, Sand Rose*
HEIGHT *3"/7.5 cm*
HABITAT *Arid regions, gravelly plains, sagebrush plains to lower mountains*
SEASON *Late May – June*

The delicate white to deep pink flowers of bitter-root close in shade and at night, but open with startling speed in sunlight. One wonders how such beauty can flourish in such poor conditions: but then, flowers bloom even in the western region of the Libyan Desert, after rain, a fact that amazed and delighted soldiers during World War II.

Lewisia honors Meriwether Lewis of the Lewis and Clark botanical expedition. In 1806 he collected a specimen in Montana (it is now that state's flower). Months after it had been pressed, he planted the desiccated root which, to everyone's astonishment, grew. Botanist Pursh promptly and aptly named the new species *rediviva* (restored to life).

Spatlum comes from an Indian name for bitter-root, which in some areas was more valued as a food source than blue camas (page 160). The orange-colored inner bark is exceedingly bitter, and both it and the red heart (the embryo of next year's flowers) were immediately removed upon digging by the Okanagan and Kootenay Indians of B.C. Flathead Indians controlled the digging grounds of the Bitterroot Valley of western Montana (disputed occasionally by the Blackfoot). The flower also gives its name to the Bitterroot Range.

This lovely flower is found in the dry interior of southern B.C., the eastern Cascades in Washington and Oregon, thence to California, and east to Montana, Colorado, and Arizona.

Linnaea borealis L. var. *longiflora* Torr.

CAPRIFOLIACEAE

TWIN-FLOWER Honeysuckle Family

OTHER NAMES *None*
HEIGHT *2"–4"/5–10 cm*
HABITAT *Woodland trails; along streams and other wet places; sea-level to about 9,000'/2,700 m*
SEASON *June – early August*

This charming flower was the favorite of Linnaeus, the botanist–classifier mentioned in 'More Than We Ever Wanted to Know About Sex' at the beginning of this book. Gronovius, one of Linnaeus's teachers, aware of his pupil's fondness for this flower, honored him by naming it *Linnaea*.

Being a circumboreal plant (*borealis*—northern, as in *aurora borealis*—northern lights), the dainty, drooping pairs of bell-shaped flowers are the same whether in Sweden or Russia, China or Alaska, Labrador or the Pacific Northwest.

Twin-flower is subtly perfumed, especially in the evening. The distinctive growth of the flowers ensures that twin-flower cannot be mistaken for any other, and even when the blooms are absent, the small evergreen leaves are easily recognized by their slightly shiny, sticky-looking blades. The fruits are sticky burrs spread by animals and humans.

A small piece of running stem, rooted at the node, will transplant to rich garden soil containing plenty of humus. Given light shade, the plant will rapidly provide a neat ground cover.

Mimulus lewisii Pursh.

SCROPHULARIACEAE

PINK MONKEY-FLOWER Figwort Family

OTHER NAMES *Lewis.' Monkey-flower, Great Purple Monkey-flower*
HEIGHT *12"–30"/30–75 cm*
HABITAT *Stream margins to mid-altitudes*
SEASON *June–July in B.C.; July–August in Alberta*

The blazing pink with yellow bee-guide (occasionally pale pink; rarely white or yellowish-white) of this monkey-flower is in striking contrast to the more usual yellow, such as those illustrated on pages 68, 70, yet the flower-form remains the same, making identification easy.

Various species of yellow-flowered mimulus are found across the four western provinces, but the one illustrated here is limited to southern B.C. and south-western Alberta. As with all the flowers in this book, this one grows also in the adjacent states of Washington and Oregon.

This and other monkey-flowers make beautiful models with which you can imitate the action triggered by a bee. The stigma (female) is equipped with clearly visible lobes that open and close like tiny hinged spoons. Take a needle and touch the lower lobe. It will close. In reality pollen scraped from a bee's tongue would then be confined in a sealed, damp chamber ideal for germination. The bee would still be looking for nectar by probing inwards and in doing so would touch the anthers (male) whose new pollen would be released onto the bee's tongue. Having fed, the bee would withdraw, but because the pollen he brought is held in the little closed spoons, there is no risk of its being deposited onto its own stigma as he brushes past it carrying pollen for a new monkey-flower. Now—and here is the miracle of an 'almost-intelligence'—you may observe that the stigma lobes of 'your' flower have reopened, because they 'realized' that your needle was phony and that you were just playing games. Had they received pollen (instead of your needle) from the same species, *they would not have reopened.*

Monarda fistulosa L. var. *menthaefolia* (Grah.) Fern.

LABIATAE

WILD BERGAMOT Mint Family

OTHER NAMES *Horse Mint, Beebalm, Lemon Mint*
HEIGHT *18"–3'/45–90 cm*
HABITAT *Medium-dry moist soil of shady creek banks, coulees, in shelter of shrubby patches giving light shade. Prairies in open woods, and mountains to about 7,000'/2,100 m*
SEASON *June–September*

Colors in this species may vary from the pink illustrated, through pinkish-mauve, and occasionally white. Bergamot is common in the dry interior of B.C., throughout the three other western Canadian provinces, and into Washington and northern Oregon.

The flowers, though small in comparison with the scarlet cultivated (now rarely wild) *M. didyma*, are nevertheless beautiful when seen as a massed group. Compare with the Canada mint on page 206 and notice the similarity of the square stems, ridged longitudinally, and the typical placement of the leaves in opposite, opposing pairs. Like all the mints, bergamot has a strong, pleasant scent that can be transmuted into a cup of tea by infusing a few crushed leaves in boiling water. At one time *M. didyma* was sold as a beverage under the name Oswego Tea.

Fistulosa means hollow, referring to the stems which are not, however, any more hollow than other mints. (For a truly hollow stem, cow parsnip on page 32 surely takes the prize.) *Menthaefolia* (*menthae*—mint, and *folia*—leaf) refers to the leaves, which resemble those of many mints. The generic name honors Nicolas Monardes (1493–1588), a Spanish botanist and physician.

B.C.'s Kootenay Indians used the plant for tea. Blackfoot tribes made an eyewash from it and the blossoms were used as a tea for stomach pains. Sioux women used the plant after confinement, and boiled leaves were applied to skin eruptions.

It is possible to transplant a small rooted stem gently taken from a large patch. Given similar soil conditions, summer moisture, and small amounts of an organic fertilizer, the plant will grow well and in a year or so will provide a taste sensation from your garden.

Petasites frigidus (L.) Fries var.
   palmatus (Ait.) Cronq.

COMPOSITAE

COLTSFOOT Composite Family

OTHER NAMES *Woodland Coltsfoot, Sweet Coltsfoot, Butterbur*
HEIGHT *4″–30″/1–9 dm*
HABITAT *Moist woods, meadows, swampy places*
SEASON *June–August*

People who have come to Canada or the U.S.A. from Europe sometimes exclaim with pleasure at finding flowers they knew in their faraway homeland, having anticipated that everything, including plants, would be different in the New World. This coltsfoot is an example; twin-flower is another: each looks the same whether in Lapland or Labrador, Sweden or Saskatchewan.

Coltsfoot flower-colors include white and (rarely) yellow. Male and female flowers are borne on separate plants (dioecious). The female bears fluffy seeds in early summer. The broad leaves are deeply lobed for at least half their length and the young ones are densely covered beneath with white, wool-like hairs, which disappear as the plant ages. As the flowers shrivel before the leaves are mature, one may fail to identify the flowers and leaves as one plant.

The species illustrated grows in Canada's four western provinces, in the West Cascade Mountains and south to northern California, together with several others, of which one, *P. sagittatus*, has leaves shaped like an arrow-head, accounting for the specific name. All species have white hairs on the under-sides of the large basal leaves.

The common name comes from the resemblance to a little colt's foot of the in-rolled leaf-shoots that follow the flower-stems in spring. The generic name is from the Greek *petasos*—a broad-brimmed hat, more or less referring to the broad leaves.

Phyllodoce empetriformis (Smith) D. Don

ERICACEAE

RED MOUNTAIN HEATH Heath Family

OTHER NAMES *Red or Purple Heather, Mountain Heath, Mountain
Heather*
HEIGHT *6″–7″/15–18 cm*
HABITAT *Mountain slopes just below timber line to high altitudes*
SEASON *Late June – early August*

The common names of this mountain plant have arisen more by association than botanical accuracy. True heaths are in the genus *Erica* (thus the
family name), and there are many garden forms known generally as 'eri-
cas'. True heather, which clothes the Scottish moorlands in August, is *Cal-
luna vulgaris*, from the Greek *kallunem*—to sweep. Brooms or besoms
were once made in heather country from the springy twigs and in Scotland
you are still likely to be described as a 'heather besom' if you are seen with
untidy hair!

This heath looks so much like a tiny conifer (fir) that it sometimes
surprises people that it flowers at all. But conifers bear cones and heathers
do not. The leaves are another instance of nature's design for water conservation: they are narrow and waxy with a groove beneath (see inset).
Red mountain heath is found in the mountains from Alaska to B.C. and
western Alberta, south to California, and in Idaho and Montana.

The Pacific Northwest has many ideal habitats for members of this
family, amazing visitors from other areas when they see the displays of
wild and cultivated flowers in their well-drained, acid environment. One
member of this interesting family is rarely recognized as a heather—the
30′/9 m arbutus tree (*Arbutus menziesii*), also called 'madrona'. It has
smooth pink or green bark, which peels in thin papery layers; panicles of
white heather-bell flowers are followed by bright orange berries. It is the
only broad-leaved evergreen tree in Canada.

Wild heaths and heathers are impossible to transplant with any hope
of blooming; even cuttings are unlikely subjects.

Plectritis congesta (Lindl.) DC.

VALERIANACEAE

SEA BLUSH Valerian Family

OTHER NAMES *Plectritis, Rosy Plectritis*
HEIGHT *1"–18"/2.5–45 cm*
HABITAT *Rock ledges above sea, short-turf meadows in sun*
SEASON *April–July*

No visitor to the west coast in springtime can fail to see and admire the huge displays of this small flower which, while humble by itself, presents a lovely pink carpet when massed, as it nearly always is, in company with buttercups and blue-eyed Marys. This species occurs in southern B.C. and Washington, in the West Cascade Mountains. A close species is found in the interior of B.C.

The generic name is thought to come from the Greek word *plektron*—plaited, referring to the densely clustered small flowers; the adjective is more or less repeated in the specific name. This is a normal occurrence in botanical naming where precise definition may be required to separate two perhaps very similar species. In this case it could be that one plectritis is less 'congested' than another.

Polygonum amphibium L.

POLYGONACEAE

WATER SMARTWEED Buckwheat Family

OTHER NAMES *Knotweed, Doorweed, Knotgrass, Water Persicaria*
HEIGHT *3″/8 cm above water level, taller on mud banks*
HABITAT *Shallow ponds and lakes, wet mud, ditches*
SEASON *June–September*

Though extremely pretty in wild ponds and shallows of lake edges, this floating plant can become a nuisance if introduced as an ornamental because seeds or rooted stems find their way into a cultivated home pool unless they are controlled in sunken pots. The fruit contains a single black seed, much liked by ducks; those they miss germinate quickly, and if allowed to grow unchecked the plant will take over, eventually smothering other plantlife by excluding light with its innumerable leaves.

If the plant is growing on land, the leaves are narrow with very short petioles, but in water they are broader and float on the surface at the end of long petioles. Air spaces inside the leaves keep them afloat and a wax coating keeps them dry.

Water smartweed is found across Canada and most of the U.S.A. There are several very similar related species: swamp smartweed (*P. coccineum*), and lady's thumb (*P. persicaria*) flourish across the prairies. Another, *P. convolvulus*, is a common weed that climbs weakly like morning glory but is less invasive.

These water plants owe their color to five sepals, there being no petals. The stems are jointed (*poly*—many, and *gonum*—joints); *amphibium* describes the plant's aquatic domicile.

Pyrola asarifolia Michx.

PYROLACEAE

LARGE WINTERGREEN Wintergreen Family

OTHER NAMES *Pink Pyrola, Alpine Pyrola, Bog Pyrola, Shinleaf,*
Liver-leaf Wintergreen
HEIGHT *12"–16"/30–40 cm*
HABITAT *Damp places, open coniferous forests, stream banks; plains*
and lower hills into mountains to 9,000'/2,700 m; aspen
bluffs
SEASON *May–September*

This is not the wintergreen used for colds in the head. Oil of wintergreen comes from false wintergreen (*Gaultheria procumbens*), which is related to the shrubby salal so common in Pacific Coast forests.

The species illustrated has its stamens hidden in a curving bunch under one petal—the uppermost. Height of the flower varies according to soil, light conditions, and aspect, and the number of blooms varies from ten to twenty-four per stem. Pyrolas will not grow anywhere but in their native habitat: they have very few feeding roots along their extensive rhizomes, and the plants form a relationship with soil fungi that cannot be duplicated in the home garden. The lifestyle of Indian pipe (page 38) makes an interesting comparison.

Several species of wintergreen may be recognized once you have an idea of the general shape and growth of the plant. The charming *P. uniflora* has a single white-to-greenish drooping flower; *P. secunda* has shining leaves and its white flowers are all turned in the same direction on one side of the stem. *P. picta* and *P. dentata* have almost green flowers. Some species are largely saprophytic, having no detectable green leaves—*P. aphylla* is one of these. *P. picta* has uniquely mottled leaves with white areas indicating lack of chlorophyll.

Pyrola is the Latin diminutive of *pyrus*—pear, referring to the leaves, some of which are somewhat pear-shaped; *asarifolia* also refers to the leaves of this species, which the botanist who named it likened to those of Asarum (wild ginger), at least in shape. Large wintergreen is common from B.C. to Manitoba and adjacent American states.

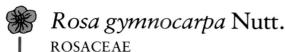

Rosa gymnocarpa Nutt.

ROSACEAE

DWARF ROSE Rose Family

OTHER NAME *Bald-hip Rose*
HEIGHT *2′–6′/6–18 dm*
HABITAT *Open woodland and coniferous forest*
SEASON *June*

The lingering perfume in summer woods is partly due to the resin-scented leaves of this our smallest rose, the diameter of which is little more than a dime. Its specific name means 'naked fruit' from the fact that, unlike many other species—including garden roses—the short sepals are shed soon after the fruit has ripened, leaving it bare and shining. The clear bright red of the hips (fruit) is visible long after the leaves have dropped.

Dwarf rose grows from B.C. south to California, in north-west Montana and western Idaho, and in north-east Oregon. B.C. Indians call it catnip tea and they also make a powder of leaves and bark to use as tobacco.

It is not surprising that roses of all descriptions have been used for centuries as decorative motifs, badges, emblems, and so on, from the red and white roses of the Houses of York and Lancaster in the fifteenth-century Wars of the Roses, to the intricately wrought gold rose that was blessed by the Pope on the fourth Sunday in Lent and presented as a form of compliment to sovereigns, cities, and other persons or institutions of the Roman Catholic faith. Some of the most famous recipients were King Henry VIII, Isabella of Spain, and Napoleon III. In modern times this beautiful ornament has been presented to the Queen of Italy (1937) and the Shrine of our Lady of Fatima (1964).

Roses, pansies, birds, and a butterfly or two—symbols of the world's frivolity—wander down the margins and around the capitals of exquisitely illuminated Books of Hours. And, to end on a rather controversial note, the Rose of Sharon of biblical fame has been accepted by botanists as a tulip common in the Holy Land (*Tulipa montana*) and not a rose at all!

Rosa nutkana Presl.

ROSACEAE

NOOTKA ROSE Rose Family

OTHER NAME *Wild Rose*
HEIGHT *2′–8′/6–24 dm*
HABITAT *Thickets and open woods*
SEASON *May–June*

Wild roses are so familiar they need no description other than to say that there are a number of western species, all deep to pale pink, sweetly scented (flower and leaves), five-petalled with bright yellow stamens arranged flatly in the center, with varying degrees of thorniness on stem and branch. One of them, *R. acicularis*, is the floral emblem of Alberta and is found also in Saskatchewan and Manitoba, and south in the mountains to Idaho, Montana (rarely), and New Mexico.

Nootka roses grow on the west coast and often in mountainous country from B.C. to northern Oregon. The bright red hips (fruit) of all wild roses, regardless of species, make good jelly and are a valuable source of vitamin C.

Literary references to roses are, of course, numerous. Shakespeare's use of the old, mellifluous name 'eglantine' ('. . . With sweet musk roses, and with eglantine'—*Midsummer Night's Dream*) reminds us that there is still a species known as *R. eglanteria*, the sweet briar found in western Washington.

Rose petals were first put to practical use in Persia (Iran) to extract the famous and expensive attar (or otto) of roses used in making perfume. This essence comes from a cultivated rose, *R. damascena*, grown today in a small area in Bulgaria known as the Valley of the Roses. Competing French perfumers once tried to grow bushes from stolen Bulgarian seeds, but failed. They tried cuttings, also to no avail. Eventually it was realized that this particular valley was the only place in Europe where these special roses would grow. During World War II the Germans forced the Bulgarians to destroy their entire crop and replace it with vegetables. It took years to recondition the altered soil for the precious roses.

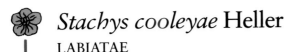 *Stachys cooleyae* Heller

LABIATAE

HEDGE NETTLE Mint Family

OTHER NAMES *Woundwort, Betony*
HEIGHT *3'–5'/9–15 dm*
HABITAT *Moist, low ground; streambanks; shady hedgerows*
SEASON *June–August*

The color of the flower illustrated here is deep magenta, but for the purpose of this book it has been classified as pink, of which magenta is a variation. This specimen was growing in sun when painted; close by was one heavily shaded by overhanging trees, a situation that resulted in washed-out color in the flowers and leaves that were greatly enlarged to catch as much light as possible. The leaves and general growth of hedge nettle look something like the well-known stinging nettle. The latter's flowers are greenish-white and the two plants are not related, nor is there any poison in the slightly hairy leaves of hedge nettle.

Hedge nettle is widespread from B.C. to southern Oregon and closely related plants are found in Alberta, Saskatchewan, and Manitoba. Marsh hedge nettle (*S. palustris*) can be recognized although it is smaller and its leaves have no stalks. It grows in the same habitat across the western provinces but only east of the Cascade Mountains in B.C.

Stachys is unaltered Greek for spike, referring to the series of whorled flowers arranged on an ascending axis. Like all the mints related to it, the stems are strongly square and the leaves hairy on both sides.

Saanich Indians drank a tea made from the roots as a spring tonic, and Haida children chewed the young stems, spitting out the fibrous part and swallowing the juice.

Trientalis latifolia Hook.

PRIMULACEAE

STARFLOWER Primrose Family

OTHER NAMES *Western or Broad-leaved Starflower*
HEIGHT *4"–8"/10–20 cm*
HABITAT *Sunny or semi-shaded woodland edges; natural openings in
      woods*
SEASON *May–June*

You may come upon wide areas covered with the broad thin leaves set in a whorl at the top of their stem, from which rise the fine, scarcely visible pedicels that carry the dainty flowers. Leaves and flowers are variable: the former may number from three to seven and reach four inches in length; the latter may have six or seven petals.

Starflower grows from tiny spindle-shaped root tubers containing edible starch, sometimes known as Indian potatoes. It is found from southern B.C. to California, and east to Alberta and Idaho.

The species illustrated should not be confused with the starflower or rock-star of the prairies, of southern B.C. to California, and of the Dakotas and Colorado, a plant of dry, rocky places. This is a member of the Saxifrage family, known as *Lithophragma bulbifera*: Greek *lithos*—stone, and *phragma*—wall. The prairie version of the flower illustrated is *T. borealis*, also called starflower: its flowers are white, rising from a whorl of five to ten leaves that are narrower than those of the pink starflower here; furthermore, it grows from creeping roots rather than tubers.

T. latifolia can be grown at home. A single tuber, taken after the flower has died, is best potted in sifted compost and sharp sand, kept moist. During winter, keep it in a cold-frame or sheltered porch where you can keep an eye on it. When the ground warms up in spring it can be transplanted to dappled shade, where it will multiply to form a charming ground cover.

Trifolium pratense L.
LEGUMINOSAE

RED CLOVER Pea Family

OTHER NAME *Trefoil*
HEIGHT *Up to 12"/30 cm*
HABITAT *Waste places, hedgerows, country roadsides, open meadows*
SEASON *May–September*

Clovers need little introduction since they abound in the countryside and even into city lots across Canada and the U.S.A. The species illustrated escaped from farm fields and became naturalized as a wild herb. It is possibly the best known of the genus because of its fat, conspicuous, bee-haunted flower and bicolored leaves divided into three (Latin *tres*—three, and *folium*—leaf; *pratense*—relating to a meadow).

Except in western Alberta this species is common in the western provinces and adjacent American states. The rounded flower head consists of fifty to 200 tiny florets that when mature produce small hard seeds relished by many birds, especially quail. The foliage is eaten by various game-birds as well as wild and domestic animals. Nodules on the roots fix nitrogen from the air, resulting in its ultimate incorporation into the soil. Cover crops of the herb are grown to be plowed under while young, as manure.

Hop clover, a tiny relative also known as yellow trefoil (*T. dubium*), annoys gardeners proud of their immaculate lawns, which it invades. Rabbit's-foot clover (*T. arvense*) has palest pink or white flowers. The famous four-leaf clover (*T. repens*) that brings Irish good luck has small white flowers. It is widespread in the Emerald Isle and in lawns elsewhere. The Irish have created a minor industry by exporting the freak leaves to Canada and the U.S.A., where they are bought by people who believe in charms. This is harmless, whether the plants are specially grown or sought in the wild, for a rare four-leaf taken from a three-leaf plant will not kill it.

BLUE

Camassia quamash (Pursh) Greene

LILIACEAE

BLUE CAMAS Lily Family

OTHER NAMES *Edible Camas, Quamash, Common Camas*
HEIGHT *9"–14"/23–35 cm*
HABITAT *Open meadows, rocky outcrops, moist depressions, low grasslands, roadsides*
SEASON *April–May*

Camas bulbs were eaten by native Indians for thousands of years before the advent of the white man and the name is, appropriately, Indian. There is another species whose virtually identical bulb is extremely poisonous. To ensure a safe harvest for the tribe the women diggers carefully weeded out the fatal death camas (page 46) while it was in bloom: edible camas flowers are blue; death camas flowers are creamy white. Just two bulbs of the latter are enough to kill you.

The edible bulbs were cooked in pits heated at the bottom by red-hot stones on which skunk-cabbage leaves, with their thick central vein removed, were layered with bulbs until the pit was full. It was topped off with soil and the whole was left to steam for several hours. Camas was also the main vegetable diet of early white settlers and trappers and possibly played a more significant part in the history of the west than any other edible plant.

Blue camas is found in B.C. from the coast to moderate elevations, and in south-western Alberta; south to northern California, east to northern Utah, Wyoming, and Montana. It grows in great profusion with the yellow western buttercup (*Ranunculus occidentalis*—page 80) and the sight of them in a meadow caused Meriwether Lewis to write in his diary in 1806: '. . . the quawmash is now in blume and from the color of its bloom at a short distance it resembles lakes of fine clear water, so complete is this deseption that on first sight I could have swoarn it was water.'

Another species (*C. leichtlinii*), also with blue flowers and edible bulbs, grows to a height of 4'/1 m in deep wet soil. This is great camas, with more and larger flowers to a stem. Its bulb lies 12"/30 cm below soil and for this reason was used as native food less than the smaller species with bulbs only 2"–6"/5–15 cm below the surface. Camas flowers begin to fade from the bottom, and the yellow anthers turn an interesting indigo blue with age. Compare with the aster on page 198, whose flowers fade from the top downwards.

Campanula rotundifolia L.

CAMPANULACEAE

HAREBELL Harebell Family

OTHER NAMES *Bluebell, Bellflower, Bluebells of Scotland, Lady's Thimble*
HEIGHT *2'/60 cm in good soil; 4"–5"/10–13 cm in mountains*
HABITAT *Prairie, sandhills, rocky outcrops and clearings; hillsides, coast, and mountains to 10,000'/3,000 m*
SEASON *June–September*

This is the bluebell of Scotland! Much confusion is caused by the use of the name bluebell: *Mertensia* is called bluebell (page 176) and the English bluebell is a hyacinth. Botanical names are clearly indispensable to identify such plants. Incidentally, harebell is a misspelling of hairbell, alluding to the fine, hair-like stems which, though delicate, are tough enough to bend but not break in the vicious winds of high mountains.

Harebells open from the top (terminal) bud first; notice how the petals are fused to form the bell (Latin *campana*—bell). The generic name comes from the diminutive noun, *campanula*—little bell. *Rotundifolia* means round-leaved, referring to the seldom seen leaves at the base of the stem (see inset); those higher up are narrow. As the flower opens the bud swings downward from its first upright position, to protect pollen and nectar from rain. Flower color varies from deep or pale blue with a touch of mauve, to pure white.

Harebell is circumboreal in distribution and is common across the western provinces and northern United States, where several other species are also found. The species extend south in the mountains as far as Texas. Some grow in wet meadows and there are several purely alpine species, all recognizable from the illustration here.

If you wish to have some in your garden, buy nursery plants; wild ones are not so easy to grow and germination periods for wild seeds are erratic. The plants like dry, sandy, or gravelly soil in full sun, although they will tolerate light shade.

Cichorium intybus L.

COMPOSITAE

CHICORY Composite Family

OTHER NAMES *Blue Sailors, Succory, Wild Endive*
HEIGHT *2'–5'/6–15 dm*
HABITAT *Roadsides, waste places, dry ditches, hedgerows, often near towns*
SEASON *July–October*

Chicory is naturalized widely in North America and is probably most prolific on the Pacific coast west of the Cascade Mountains. It is a plant that almost dramatically illustrates the workings of the biological clock synchronization between flower and pollinator. Chicory opens its nectaries at about seven o'clock in the morning and closes them again at noon. During this period scores of insects—particularly bees—can be seen swarming to feed at the lovely blue blossoms. The bar closes at noon, but this does not imply that the flower petals fold, although they will do so on a cloudy day. It only means that the production of nectar is at its peak in that period.

Common plant names alter remarkably little over the centuries and some are unchanged from the antique languages, chicory included: *cichorium*—endive, chicory, is Latin derived from the Greeks, who probably took it from Arabic, for this plant was known to the Egyptians. The specific name is Latin *intibus, intubus, or intybus*—endive or succory (another name for chicory). It is a relative of the bobbin-shaped salad endive (*C. endivia*). Both have blue flowers, which are 'perfect' (bear only ray flowers, which carry both stamen and pistil).

Chicory root is still roasted and ground for use as an addition to coffee, and the basal leaves, which are large and resemble dandelion leaves, may be cooked as a vegetable. The roots, grated and added to boiling water and then steeped and strained, make a tonic and can be used for liver and rheumatic complaints.

Chicory has made its way into some rather indifferent eighteenth-century poetry, the most quotable being that of John Gay (who wrote *The Beggar's Opera*); in 'The Shepherd's Week' he wrote:

Upon her grave the rosemary they threw
The daisy, butter-flower and endive blue.

Collinsia parviflora Lindl.

SCROPHULARIACEAE

BLUE-EYED MARY Figwort Family

OTHER NAMES *Bluelips, Small-flowered Blue-eyed Mary*
HEIGHT *2"–10"/5–25 cm*
HABITAT *Moderately moist open woodlands, roadsides, mossy rocks,*
open grassy places; sea level to 7,500'/2,200 m
SEASON *April–July*

This little annual is not very significant (*parviflora* means 'small flow-ered'), but what it lacks in size it makes up for in charm, its pale mauve upper lips and corolla tube (note the curious kink in it) contrasting against the royal blue of the lower lip. It is common from Alaska to southern Cali-fornia, and across the prairie lands of Canada and the U.S.A.

Another blue-eyed Mary with larger but exactly similar flowers grows in southern B.C. west of the Cascade Mountains, and on to California. *C. grandiflora* and *C. parviflora* are easily distinguishable by size alone.

These little plants must renew themselves annually before winter moisture has drained away or evaporated. They flourish in almost any soil, including dry hillsides, blooming and setting seed in a few weeks. The seeds lie dormant through the winter and germinate as soon as the snow melts in the following spring.

Compare this tiny member of the figwort family with some of its rela-tives such as the penstemon (page 208), or mimulus (pages 68, 70). The flower forms place them unmistakably in the figwort family: five petals joined to create a tube.

The generic name for the flower illustrated was given to honor an American botanist, Zacheus Collins (1764–1831).

You will usually find small-flowered blue-eyed Mary growing with buttercups and, on the Pacific coast, with pink sea-blush (page 142).

Delphinium nuttallianum Pritz.

RANUNCULACEAE

LARKSPUR Buttercup Family

OTHER NAME *Delphinium*
HEIGHT *18"–24"/45–60 cm*
HABITAT *Sagebrush desert to mountain valleys and slopes, especially ponderosa pine belt, in well drained, gravelly soil*
SEASON *May–July*

All delphiniums have the same flower form and general habit of growth, despite wide variations in height, and anything from three to fifteen flowers to a stem; some are as tall and stately as the well-known annual larkspurs and perennial delphiniums. Colors (in other species) may be blue, violet, purple, pink, white, blue-and-white, or cream. The species illustrated makes a spectacular sight when seen *en masse* in south-western B.C., the southern Cascade Mountains to northern California, the Columbia River Gorge, east to Alberta, Montana, Wyoming, and Nebraska, south to Colorado and Arizona and in the northern Sierra Nevadas. There are many more species of larkspur distributed through the prairie provinces and adjacent American states. All are extremely poisonous to cattle, although oddly enough sheep do not seem to be affected.

Delphinium was used as a flower name in the first century AD by Dioscorides, a Greek physician. It comes from *delphin*, or the Latinized form *delphinus*—dolphin, from the supposed resemblance of the long spur (the nectary) to that intelligent mammal. The common name probably refers to the long hind toe of the horned and other larks which, being ground walkers and not perching birds, require the additional toe-length for balance. Larkspur in profile can easily be imagined as a bird's foot.

The insets show, clockwise: a stamen, upper petal, lower petal, hairy back of a sepal.

Wild delphiniums can be raised from *newly ripened* seeds planted outdoors in midsummer into rich humus-filled soil in full sun. Stake the tall varieties.

Gentiana sceptrum Griseb.

GENTIANACEAE

BOTTLE GENTIAN Gentian Family

OTHER NAMES *Swamp Gentian, Closed Gentian, Stiff Gentian*
HEIGHT *8"–20"/20–50 cm*
HABITAT *Meadows and boggy lake margins*
SEASON *July–October*

The glorious royal blue of this rather tall gentian is found on the west side of the Cascade Mountains in B.C. and south to north-west California. The prairie provinces in Canada and adjacent American states have other species that closely resemble the one illustrated.

The bottle-shaped flowers never fully open, merely turning purple with age, so that two of its common names are apt, and of the ten to fifteen pairs of leaves, the lowest are reduced to short clasping bracts (see inset).

Gentians vary in size, form, and color, some being nearly prostrate with large, single, tube flowers lying almost parallel to the ground; others, like the one illustrated, are tall and stiff. An identifying feature is the tiny fold in each petal that gives gentian flowers a sculptured look (see inset).

Two other species with deep blue flowers are common to the prairies and elsewhere, including southern B.C. to California and Arizona: *G. affinis* is found in sandy areas and in moist, even saline meadows; *G. andrewisii*, with flowers similar in shape to *G. sceptrum*, clustered at the top of the stems, grows in wet meadows. A third has shaded, separated petals, each with a fine fringe, and is known as fringed gentian (*G. crinita*). Gentians are difficult to establish in a home garden unless purchased as nursery plants. *G. crinita* can only be started from seed.

Gentiana is from the name of an ancient king, Gentius; *sceptrum* is Latin for a scepter. The plant was first recorded by the Anglo-Saxons. (c. AD 1000), who called it feldwyrt (*feld*—field, and *wyrt*—root). 'Wyrt' eventually became 'wort', meaning a plant, as in figwort.

Gentians contain bitter alkaloids, which are extracted for use as tonics. *G. lutea* is the official gentian that yields the substance; and *G. amarella,* a North American species, also provides a bitter tonic (Latin *amarus*—bitter).

Linum Lewisii Pursh
LINACEAE

LEWIS WILD FLAX Flax Family

OTHER NAME *Wild Blue Flax*
HEIGHT *8″–24″/20–60 cm*
HABITAT *Dry prairie flats; subalpine ridges*
SEASON *May–July*

That Lewis Flax is a perennial herb is implied in one of its synonyms, *L. perenne* L. Some botanists consider these as separate species, based on minute differences in pistil and stamen lengths, but let us not quibble! Wild flax is common on plains, hillsides, and mountain slopes across the southern prairies, into B.C. and the western states south of the border. The flowers are borne on very slender stems, which nod and dance with every breath of air. The color is sky-blue—rare in the mountains, where blue tends to be mauve or purple (see the so-called blue clematis on page 204). Each delicate petal of flax is veined in a deeper shade of cobalt blue. On first opening in the morning the blossoms are funnel-shaped; they flatten as the day progresses and are dropped the following day, leaving a spherical green seed capsule. The seeds contain oil and when wet produce clear mucilage. The linseed oil of commerce, however, comes from *L. usitatissimum*, a cultivated annual.

There are several other species of wild flax, some with yellow, pink, white, or red flowers. All have the characteristic delicacy of nodding blooms, straplike smooth gray-green alternate leaves, and round seed capsules.

Linum, as flax is often called, is an ancient plant whose name is variously attributed to the Greek word *linon*—a thread, or to the Celtic *lin* with the same meaning. Either way the plant gives us fiber to make linen, especially in Ireland. It is woven into fine quality cloth from coarse to gossamer fine and it lasts 'forever'. I inherited a bedsheet hand-embroidered with the date 1825. It became in turn a tablecloth, napkins, and ended as dishcloths in 1950!

For centuries Egyptian cotton made from this humble plant clothed the Pharaohs, the priests, and the common man. Flax-seed capsules were found in a tomb dating back to 3100 BC, perhaps put there to ensure a continuing supply of thread in the next world.

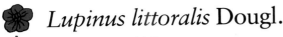

Lupinus littoralis Dougl.

LEGUMINOSAE

LUPINE Pea Family

OTHER NAMES *None*
HEIGHT *3"–3'/7.5–90 cm*
HABITAT *Coastline, near shore*
SEASON *May–June*

The lupine illustrated is one of many beautiful species, nearly all blue (although a pure yellow occurs on Vancouver Island, B.C.); Alberta, Saskatchewan, and Manitoba have four lupines, recognizable from this painting. *L. littoralis* grows throughout coastal B.C. and south to northern California.

As with other members of the pea family, lupines have nitrogen-stabilizing bacteria in tiny root-nodules which help to enrich poor soil and, if plowed under while young, also provide humus. But the plants are poisonous to cattle and sheep, and children should not be allowed to eat the seeds.

Ancient seeds are a fascinating subject. In 1954 a mining engineer in the Yukon was digging through frozen silt when he came upon some ancient collared lemming burrows in which he found a hoard of large seeds. Out of curiosity he bottled some and kept them on his office desk for twelve years until someone realized their significance. The seeds were sent to the National Museum of Canada where, after carbon dating, some were placed on damp filter paper. Six germinated within forty-eight hours. A year later one plant produced mature flowers. It was the arctic lupine (*L. arcticus*), a species still common on tundra and in subalpine forests, but these seeds were between 10,000 and 15,000 years old—8,000 years older than the oldest known seed, that of a sacred lotus, which had germinated after lying dormant for 2,000 years in a far-Eastern peat bog.*

Roots of the lupine illustrated were eaten just before bedtime by Haida and Kwakiutl Indians, because the raw roots contain compounds that cause drowsiness and dizziness. It is one of the plants that were introduced into England by the explorer–botanist David Douglas.

The generic name *Lupinus* comes from the Latin *lupus*—wolf. The origin is obscure but is thought to mean that, because lupines grow in poor soil, they 'devour' the nutrients, whereas in fact lupines help to enrich it, as explained briefly above. The specific name *littoralis* or *litoralis* means 'relating to a shore'.

*PORSILD, A.E., et al.: *Lupinus arcticus* Wats. Grown from Seeds of Pleistocene Age. *Science*, Vol. 158, p. 113, Oct. 6, 1967.

Mertensia longiflora Greene

BORAGINACEAE

BLUEBELLS Borage Family

OTHER NAMES *Lungwort, Long-flowered Bluebells, Mertensia*
HEIGHT *6"–8"/15–20 cm*
HABITAT *Ponderosa pine-sagebrush flats; dry hillsides*
SEASON *April–June*

Here is an instance in which you need to 'have the Latin'. The common names are utterly confusing. Bluebells make one think of Scotland (whose native 'bluebell' is a harebell or campanula, illustrated on page 162); or of English 'bluebells', which are hyacinths. Lungwort belongs to the genus *Pulmonaria* and is no relation. *Mertensia* was coined for F.C. Mertens, a late-eighteenth century German botanist, and *longiflora* means having a long flower (the corolla).

A very close relative, *M. oblongifolia*, can be distinguished by its shorter corolla tubes and long-stemmed, pointed basal leaves, which are rarely present in flowering plants of *M. longiflora*. The former plant grows from fairly stout rootstock lying deeper in the soil than the shallow, easily detached, tuberous root of *M. longiflora*. There are several species of *Mertensia*, one of which (*M. paniculata*) may reach five feet. All have blue, tubular flowers which turn pink as they age, and are arranged as illustrated.

M. longiflora grows from the dry southern interior of B.C. to central Oregon, east of the Cascade Mountains, occasionally to north-eastern California; east to north-western Montana (west of the continental divide) and to Boise, Idaho. *M. oblongifolia* has much the same range and includes central Nevada and northern Utah. *M. paniculata*, whose preferred habitat is along stream banks and other moist places to high mountains, occurs in the Pacific Northwest in the Olympic Mountains, from B.C. to Washington and in the prairie provinces. The very similar *M. bella* is found in the mountains of south-western Oregon and in Idaho.

Mertensias can be moved by root division or propagation by seed; those found east of the Cascade Mountains, however, can only be grown in that region.

Veronica americana Schwein, ex Benth.

SCROPHULARIACEAE

AMERICAN SPEEDWELL Figwort Family

OTHER NAME *Brooklime*
HEIGHT *6″–12″/15–30 cm, sometimes to 36″/90 cm*
HABITAT *Pond shores, damp ditches, streambanks, swamps*
SEASON *May–August*

'God speed you well' is the old English meaning of the common name. This flower is also named for St Veronica and through her is credited with miraculous powers of healing, even the dread scrofula, or King's Evil. Such powers are attributed to other members of the family as well, thus the family name *Scrophulariaceae*. Brooklime is from 'a brook', and from the verb 'to lime', a horrible practice of trapping birds with a sticky substance. Since this was often done near water, the little blue flower became associated with muddy places and trapped birds.

The plant is found from B.C. to Manitoba, south to California, and east across most of the U.S.A.

The charming little clear blue flowers are very delicate, and drop at the slightest touch. The two stamens and stigma repay examination with a hand lens (see inset). Weak, thin-leaved stems stand upright until they reach 10″–12″/26–30 cm, when further growth becomes horizontal, frequently right into water, where they are again held upright.

Another veronica (*V. chamaedrys*) invades lawns through much of the north-west—albeit charmingly—with blue half-inch flowers almost flat on the ground. As there are more than 200 species in the temperate areas of North America, you will doubtless find many more once you have identified a growing specimen with the illustration here.

PURPLE TO MAUVE

Erigeron filifolius Nutt.

COMPOSITAE

FLEABANE Composite Family

OTHER NAMES *Daisy, Erigeron, Thread-leaf Fleabane*
HEIGHT *12"/30 cm*
HABITAT *Dry plains and foothills, often with sagebrush*
SEASON *June–August*

This is an old plant in more ways than one: the Greeks named the genus (*eri*—early, or spring; and *geron*—old man). The Roman naturalist Pliny the Elder refers to it in one of his thirty-seven volume works (the poor chap was killed when Mount Vesuvius buried Pompeii in AD 79) and in 1601 his words were translated by Philemon Holland as '. . . it looketh hoarie like an old graybeard.' True enough, some fleabanes produce seed-heads early in the year and some of the spring-flowering species do have a rather tatterdemalion appearance when they should be looking young and spruce. Thus a geriatric flower!

Fleabane is larger than the common daisy of the front lawn but is often confused with aster, which blooms later in the summer. Fleabane petals are more numerous and narrower than those of aster. Colors vary from white through cream to pink, mauve, or purple.

About 135 species are native to North America, from the plains to the Rocky Mountains, with more than thirty for the prairie lands. The one illustrated grows from southern B.C. to north-west Montana, south to the East Cascade Mountains, to northern California, and east through the Snake River Plains almost as far as Wyoming.

The species *E. canadensis* is still referred to as containing a volatile oil useful for diarrhea and kidney troubles, because of its astringent and diuretic properties.

The common name is also old, being bestowed when the plant was thought to discourage fleas.

Listera cordata (L.) R. Br.

ORCHIDACEAE

HEART-LEAVED TWAYBLADE Orchid Family

OTHER NAMES *Heart-leaves, Mannikin Twayblade*
HEIGHT *4″–10″/10–25 cm*
HABITAT *Mossy bogs, cold swamps; damp, mossy coniferous forests*
SEASON *May–July*

The illustration is an enlargement and the inset of a single bloom is multiplied by ten (the live flower petals are about ¹/₁₆″/3mm long). Finding this minute orchid is quite a challenge, especially as it grows half-submerged in moss. It is found in suitable habitats across Canada to Newfoundland, in Alaska, and south to California, New Mexico, and North Carolina. This little orchid has two color-forms: the purple (illustrated) and a greenish-yellow.

Under a hand lens the blossom shows unexpected iridescent surfaces of mauve, green, and yellow stripes. The distinguishing feature is the lip, which is deeply cleft and has a small hook at the end of each projecting strand. The shape of the two leaves and the common name are clarified in the species name: Latin *cordus*—heart; also *tway*—two, and *blade*—leaf.

Twayblade has an astonishing method of pollination and an almost military precision in timing between arrival and departure of an insect. When the beak-like projection of the flower column is touched, a drop of viscous fluid is expelled which glues the crumbly pollen (pollinia) to the insect.

Space does not permit discussion here, but the reader who would like to know more about the orchid's ways of avoiding self-pollination might like to read B.J.D. Meeuse's account in *The Story of Pollination* (see Selected References, p. 235).

Orobanche uniflora L. var. *purpurea* (Heller) Achey
OROBANCHACEAE

ONE-FLOWERED CANCER-ROOT

Broomrape Family

OTHER NAME *Broomrape*
HEIGHT *2"–4"/5–10 cm*
HABITAT *Waste places open to sun; damp woods or grassy areas*
SEASON *April–May on west coast; June–August on prairie*

Broomrape has been around a long time: in Europe a species (*Rapum genistae*) was known in 1578 to be a parasite on roots of broom (genista), furze (gorse), clover, and other legumes; hence broomrape, despite the fact that *rapum* means a turnip. In 1671 it became *Orobanche major* (yet another, *O. minor*, was introduced to North America). Of *O. major* it was said that '. . .it easeth the pains in the reins' (kidneys). Eliza Doolittle might have stolen the line!

The derivation of the genus name accurately reflects the plant's function: Greek *orobos*—vetch, or clinging plant, and *ancho*—to strangle. *Uniflora* means one flower. By whichever name you call it, the species illustrated is a parasite upon the roots of quite specific plants. You may find it growing close to members of the genus *Mimulus*, with sea-blush and blue-eyed Mary (pages 70, 142, 166), but it is not parasitical on them. It chooses instead the stonecrops and saxifrages, or flowers in the composite family such as dandelion or daisy. Being a parasite, cancer-root has no leaves or even vestiges of leaves but rises directly from the soil (see also Indian pipe, page 38).

The genus is widespread from B.C. to Manitoba, from sea-level and the plains to submontane elevations. *O. uniflora* grows in B.C. and Alberta; two more very similar cancer-roots are found across the four western provinces: one of them has from one to ten flowers in a group and may vary from purple to yellowish; the other is purple with rather stout, slightly sticky pink stems 2"–10"/5–25 cm high. A rare yellow form in B.C. is parasitic on coniferous tree roots (*O. pinorum*).

Pinguicula vulgaris L.

LENTIBULARIACEAE

BUTTERWORT Bladderwort Family

OTHER NAME *Bog Violet*
HEIGHT *1"–5"/2.5–13 cm*
HABITAT *Bogs or mires; wet soil in mountains; stream margins*
SEASON *May–August according to elevation*

At first glance a patch of these dainty flowers, which may be anything from two or three flowers to an area colored purple for ten yards, may be mistaken for violets, but if you look again you will notice several differences. The thick, soft leaves are a strangely livid yellow-green and grow in a ground-hugging rosette; they are slimy and their edges roll inward, quite unlike the violet's heart-shaped, often hairy leaf. A straight spur is attached to the upper surface of the corolla and the five-part calyx has three lobes facing towards the petals, two backwards towards the tip of the spur.

Butterwort is a carnivorous plant whose leaves trap small insects (mostly midges) on their greasy surfaces; the leaf-edges roll inward onto the living creature trapped there. Protein is dissolved and absorbed by the plant's digestive enzymes, providing nitrogen lacking in the leached acid soil of its boggy habitat.

This flower is circumboreal in distribution from Alaska southwards into the mountains of B.C., Washington, and Oregon, northern Minnesota and northern Vermont, across the northern parts of the Canadian Prairie provinces and into northern Quebec, north-central Labrador, and Newfoundland.

The Latin name comes from *pinguis* meaning 'fat' (the greasy-looking leaves), and *vulgaris* meaning 'common'. It is not, however, nearly as common as its name implies. The common name also picks up the greasy theme, and 'wort' is Middle English for plant.

Butterwort is delicate and difficult to transplant. Like most bog plants it demands very special conditions. In its native habitats a substratum of calcareous rock usually lies beneath the layer of acid topsoil or mud; it prefers the moisture of a mire rather than the perpetually sodden mud of a true bog, where there is no drainage.

Another example of a carnivorous plant is the sundew, one of which you will find on page 18.

Potentilla palustris (L.) Scop.

ROSACEAE

SWAMP CINQUEFOIL Rose Family

OTHER NAMES *Marsh Five-finger, Purple Cinquefoil*
HEIGHT *8″–18″/20–45 cm*
HABITAT *Shallow water and bogs*
SEASON *May–July*

Look closely for this interesting flower when you are canoeing round the shallow edges of some quiet lake, or exploring a bog or swamp. The roots in the bottom mud are long, smooth rhizomes that send up one to nine flowering stems and dark green leaves, silvery on the back, deeply toothed and arranged in leaflets numbering three to seven, often edged with purple. Each stem bears one to three flowers which rise above the water: since this is usually dark brown peat water, the flowers are inconspicuous.

Cinquefoil's name comes from the French *cinq*—five, and *feuille*—leaf, and the flowers are mostly yellow. *P. palustris* differs from all other members of the genus *Potentilla*, having purple flowers. The five (occasionally six) sepals are somewhat leaf-like, green outside and purple within. The petals are very small, pointed, and dark red, placed between the sepals. As the pollen ripens, its bright yellow creates an aureole of contrast with the deep purple anthers. And here is one of those exceptions I mentioned in the introductory section (page XII)—a member of the rose family that may carry six instead of the usual five petals and sepals.

Swamp cinquefoil is a common circumboreal plant that can be found in suitable habitats from coast to coast across Canada and the northern and central United States, and also in Greenland and Eurasia.

Prunella vulgaris L.

LABIATAE

SELF-HEAL Mint Family

OTHER NAMES *Heal-all, Carpenter-weed*
HEIGHT *3″–12″/7.5–30 cm*
HABITAT *Roadsides, forest edges, ditches; open woods; wet places and hedges; sea level to moderate altitudes*
SEASON *May–October*

'He needs neither physician nor surgeon that hath self-heal and to help himself.' This old German saying refers to an epidemic disease of the tongue and throat suffered in the sixteenth century when the tongue was covered with a brown crust (German *die braune*—brown). Self-heal is quoted as being specifically used to cure the patients, mostly soldiers. Its old name was 'brunella', diminutive of the Latin *brunus*—brown, but it is now less correctly known as 'prunella', though the old generic title is being restored in English floras. The plant was known long before all this, being mentioned in 1387 as a healing herb. Even today an infusion of leaves and flowers is useful taken internally for bleeding and as a gargle for sore throats.

The ridged, squarish stems help place this very common flower in the mint family, as does the prominent lip of the flower itself. The flower-head is easily distinguished by its squared-off pyramid shape and bright purple petals setting the plant off against the leaves of other plants: sometimes the lower lip is white, and one may occasionally find a pale pink flower (or, rarely, a pure white). Unlike mint, self-heal has no perfume.

Native and introduced populations of self-heal abound in Canada and the United States.

Anemone patens L. var. *multifida* Pritzel

RANUNCULACEAE

PRAIRIE CROCUS Buttercup Family

OTHER NAMES *Anemone, Pasqueflower, Windflower, Prairie Smoke,*
  Blue Tulip
HEIGHT *2″–16″/5–40 cm*
HABITAT *Open slopes, dry prairie grassland and open woods, moderate*
  to high altitudes (about 9,000′/2,700 m)
SEASON *Low elevations—early March; higher levels—June*

True harbingers of spring, these soft mauve (occasionally white) flowers rise directly from the cold ground, often close to lingering snow patches. The leaves appear later. The whole plant is covered with fine white silky hairs, and the leaves, when they unfold after the flower has faded, are deeply cut and feathery. The flower is replaced by a beautiful fluffy seed-head, each seed (achene) having a long white filament. Air currents carry the mature plumed achenes considerable distances before they settle on the earth to start a new colony. You will find other filamented achenes in this book, such as mountain avens, milkweed, and wild blue clematis.

This well-known and much-loved flower is widespread from B.C. to Manitoba, where it is the provincial floral emblem. It is a marvellous thing to see these anemones growing in the prairie regions in vast sheets of mauve as far as the eye can see. The flowers can also be found from Alaska to the Wenatchee Mountains, south through Montana to Texas and east to Illinois.

Anemos means 'wind' in Greek, hence one of the common names. Pasqueflower relates to the Passion since it blooms about Eastertime (French *pâque*—Easter).

Like other members of the buttercup family, anemone leaves contain a chemical that causes blisters. Blackfoot and Kootenay Indians bound the leaves over boils and sores for a short time to draw out infection. Sheep may be poisoned by eating them on overgrazed land.

Speaking of the anemone prompts me to digress wildly and, for the sake of general interest, to mention a biblical flower.

Speculation, argument and counter-argument have gone on for centuries over the identity of the most famous flower in the Bible, the 'lily of the field'. Many different flowers have been dubbed 'lilies'.

Although there were naturalists, even botanists, before and shortly after the time of Christ (Aristotle and Pliny, to name but two), early writers had no specialized knowledge of plants and assumed that the flowers they saw growing in Europe were also growing in the Holy Land, which *was* true of some species. Only in recent times have professional botanists arrived at reasonably valid conclusions by comparing many translations of

the Bible with on-the-spot observations of plants in that part of the world.

Let me encapsulate two opposed versions, each valid, each speculative, since nobody will ever really know . . .

It has been established that in biblical days there were only two true lilies in Palestine: *L. chalcedonicum*—scarlet martagon, said to be common by some authorities, uncommon according to others, and *L. candidum*—Madonna lily, a doubtful second since it was a cultivated species that escaped to the wild and therefore was probably not native.

The flower accepted by most authorities is an anemone (*A. coronaria*), which is also called windflower and which we know as a garden anemone (*A. St Brigid* or *A. de Caen*). It is so common in the Holy Land, especially in the scarlet color, that it 'clothes the land of Israel in spring' and is as abundant today on the plains, the lush shores of the Lake of Galilee, and on the Mount of Olives as it undoubtedly was in Jesus' time. It is felt that this flower is the obvious choice, since Jesus always took for His parables an object familiar in the daily life of His listeners and would have been looking at masses of these lovely, many-colored blooms as He spoke.

But then there is the counter-argument put forward by Dr Ephraim

Ha-Reubeni, Professor of Biblical Botany at the Hebrew University of Jerusalem. Contrary to the belief of every writer and painter that the 'lily of the field' was a spectacular bloom such as the anemone, he maintains that it was a flower whose innate, humble beauty had to be carefully pointed out to make the point that '. . . even Solomon in all his glory was not arrayed like one of these'. Quoting the passage farther in support of his theory—'. . . if God so clothe the grass of the field, which today is, and tomorrow is cast into the oven . . .'—the professor holds that Christ was referring to a chamomile flower (*Anthemis palaestina*), a small, very common daisy that would have been gathered with the dried grass *and cast into the oven*. Since chamomile blooms later and lasts longer than the anemone, it would be more likely to be present at the time of hay gathering.

This theory seems to me more valid, since dried grass was (and sometimes still is) used in the Middle East for rapid heating of the sunken, clay baking ovens until they are hot enough to cook the thin sheets of unleavened bread. But one may confidently expect that botanical scholars will not allow the matter to rest there!

Aster eatonii (Gray) Howell

COMPOSITAE

ASTER Composite Family

OTHER NAME *Michaelmas Daisy*
HEIGHT *20"–40"/5–10 dm*
HABITAT *Roadsides, open woodlands, lakeshores, seashore*
SEASON *July–October*

One or more species of aster is to be found in every province in Canada from temperate to subarctic regions. There are about 300 in North America, and nineteen of them are found on the Canadian prairie. The one illustrated ranges from southern B.C. to south-eastern Saskatchewan, with close species in Manitoba. Aster colors may be mauve, purple, pink, or white; the leaves range from narrow (as in the illustration) to large and oval. There is a yellow variety in Manitoba (*A. ptarmicoides* var. *lutescens*), and several montane and dwarf alpine species, which bloom from June to August.

Asters, whose flowers bloom and die from the top downwards, look rather like fleabanes (in the same family), except that the latter bloom in early summer and have fifty or more ray florets, whereas asters have ten to fifty, and although the peak blooming season is from mid-August to September, they may linger into November in favorable locations. Wild and cultivated asters are much loved by butterflies.

The name in English, Latin, and Greek means a star. Michaelmas daisy comes to us from the sixteenth century, when Pope Gregory XIII's revised calendar caused Michaelmas Day (September 29) to fall ten days earlier, a period when asters are in full bloom in many gardens.

Cirsium arvense (L.) Scop.

COMPOSITAE

CANADA THISTLE Composite Family

OTHER NAMES *Cursed Thistle, Creeping Thistle*
HEIGHT *2'–5'/6–15 dm*
HABITAT *Hedgerows, roadsides, wild and cultivated fields; sea-level to 7,500'/2,250 m*
SEASON *June–August*

Although the common name implies that this is a native plant, it was in fact introduced from Europe, Asia, and North Africa and was naturalized across western North America. From its other names one understands the exasperation of farmer and gardener whose land is overrun, often to the point of no return, by this beautiful but noxious weed. It is extremely hardy; creeping roots lie deep enough in the soil to obtain moisture in the driest weather, and when the cultivator turns them up the chopping action ensures still further multiplication. Yet the plant nourishes many butterflies, is loved by honey-bees, and in late summer provides seeds for birds, especially American goldfinches (English goldfinches are also known as thistle-birds).

Unlike most other thistles, this one bears male and female flowers on different plants (dioecious).

Cirsium comes from the Greek *kirsos*—a swollen vein, for which thistles were used as a remedy.

The well-known heraldic emblem of Scotland is *Onopordon acanthium*, a thistle similar to the *Cirsium* genus.

Cirsium undulatum (Nutt.) Spreng.
COMPOSITAE

WAVY-LEAF THISTLE Composite Family

OTHER NAME *Woolly Thistle*
HEIGHT *1'–7'/3–21 dm*
HABITAT *Dry prairies and roadsides*
SEASON *May–September*

Unlike its relative the Canada thistle (page 200), this is a native plant common, but not abundant, in western Canada and the United States, to Mexico. It is found in dry interior locations rather than on the coast. Pink, purple, mauve, or white thistle flowers are very beautiful and it seems a pity that in some areas people are required by municipal authorities to destroy the plants as noxious weeds or at least to chop off the flowers to prevent them from setting seed. One is constantly torn between love of wildflowers (and of all the creatures they nourish) and one's civic obligation to maintain a weed-free garden.

In its first year this particular thistle does not flower, and the taproots during this phase were once dug, roasted, and eaten by Interior B.C. Indians, who also used them as a poultice for toothache. The 'down' can be used to light fires, as it ignites even from a spark from an empty cigarette lighter.

The generic name is explained under *C. arvense* (page 200), and the specific *undulatum* rather obviously means wavy.

Thistles are ancient weeds that plagued farmers as much in biblical times as today, and there are several references to them in the Old Testament and at least one in the New Testament.

Clematis columbiana (Nutt.) T. & G.

RANUNCULACEAE

BLUE CLEMATIS Buttercup Family

OTHER NAME *Purple Virgin's Bower*
HEIGHT *Prostrate or climbing to 20'/6 m*
HABITAT *Open woods and talus slopes; shady mountain slopes; valleys*
SEASON *May–July*

Of several wild clematis species the one illustrated is easily the most beautiful. It is by no means common, even though its range is wide. There are differences of opinion as to color, but to me it is a long way from purple, and I have placed it half-way between blue and purple, which is mauve.

Blue clematis is found from B.C. to northern Oregon, east to Alberta and in Montana and Wyoming. Similar purple species are found in Alberta and Saskatchewan. Authorities differ on the presence of a purple clematis in Manitoba, some saying that *C. verticillaris* is found, while another states that it has been reported but not seen—in other words it is not 'official'. In any event it is rare.

Clematis 'petals' are really colored sepals. The species illustrated bears exquisite white, emerald-tipped stamens. Some of these may look like very narrow petals (petaloid) but they are still stamens, although sterile. When the seeds (achenes) mature, the flower-head is transformed into a delicate ball of pale mauve (later white) fluff, each achene having a feathery 'tail' (known as a persistent style) to aid it in becoming airborne and transported by the wind until it lands and, ideally, germinates. You may find blue clematis trailing its woody stems down a slope, climbing by its leaf-tendrils upon itself or on other herbs or shrubs or along fences. The leaflets are in threes but it is the flower you must look for, as the vine is inconspicuous among the greens of other plants.

The wild clematis are in the same genus as those we know in gardens. The word comes from the Greek *klema*, meaning tendril. Incidentally, the word clematis is pronounced with a short 'e', with the accent on the first syllable, as in temple. Too often it is spoken as clemātis. After greenhouse germination from fresh wild seed, the little plant, like all its relatives, likes its feet in the shade and its head in the sun or dappled shade.

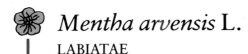

Mentha arvensis L.

LABIATAE

CANADA MINT Mint Family

OTHER NAMES *Field Mint, Wild Mint, Corn Mint*
HEIGHT *8"–20"/20–51 cm*
HABITAT *Streambanks, lakeshores, damp meadows*
SEASON *July – early September*

This mint might be called the poor relation of the more dazzling bergamot (page 136), but what it lacks in beauty it makes up in usefulness. Tea made from it, alone or with lavender, rosemary, and bergamot, is pleasant on hot days or for upset stomach and nausea. In fact all the members of this large family (some 3,500 species with world-wide distribution) can be used to make tea, the active element being the oil contained in hundreds of tiny glands in the leaves. Four species are natural (Canada mint, pennyroyal, spearmint, and apple-scented mint); all the others are cultivated hybrids.

Pennyroyal is attractive in garden areas where grass does not flourish; once established it can be lightly mown and provides its refreshing perfume whenever it is trodden on, which bears out the following legend of the generic name. Minthe was the mistress of Pluto, king of the underworld, whose jealous queen Persephone, goddess of spring, transformed her into a low-growing plant to be crushed underfoot forever. To mitigate this awful fate Pluto ordained that she would forever be remembered by decreeing that the more Minthe was trampled upon the sweeter it would smell. The specific name *arvensis* is Latin for field.

Examine a single flower with your hand-lens and you will see that whereas from a distance it appeared to have four petals, in fact the top two are joined, with a slit at the tip. Mints have the distinctive lower lip, which is described in the family name *Labiatae*, from Latin *labia*—lip. The square stem is typical of the family, as are the paired leaves growing in opposite directions. Plants outside the mint family may also have square stems but they also have other, different characteristics.

Penstemon fruticosus (Pursh) Greene var. *scouleri* (Lindl.) Cronq.

SCROPHULARIACEAE

SHRUBBY PENSTEMON Figwort Family

OTHER NAMES *Shrubby Beardtongue, Mayflower, Pride-of-the-Mountain*
HEIGHT *6"–12"/15–30 cm*
HABITAT *Foothills to 10,000'/3,000 m on steep road-cuts; rocky, open places in poor, gravelly soil*
SEASON *May–July*

Bewildering numbers and forms of penstemon grow wild in North America (116 species are listed for the Pacific Northwest alone); many have been cultivated and are garden favorites. The one illustrated is rather woody (*fruticosus*—shrubby) and lends itself well to rooting at home from short cuttings planted in gritty soil. The large tubular flowers of this species cover enormous areas of open spaces, creating a sea of pale mauve.

Penstemons are related to flowers like the mimulus (pages 68, 70, 134), all having five petals partially fused into a tube, with considerable color and other variations in the different genera.

Penstemon (sometimes spelled pentstemon) comes from the Greek words *pente*—five, and *stemon*—thread, hence five stamens, one of which lacks an anther and is therefore sterile (see inset).

Shrubby penstemon grows widely in southern B.C., Alberta, Washington, and Montana, and south to central Oregon and Wyoming. Many others grow in Saskatchewan and Manitoba and adjoining states in the U.S.A., varying from large-flowered to small, and colored white, yellow, lilac, blue, or purple.

Thompson Indians called shrubby penstemon 'hummingbird's sucking substance', the same name they used for Indian paintbrush, which is in the same family.

Phacelia linearis (Pursh) Holz.

HYDROPHYLLACEAE

NARROW-LEAVED PHACELIA Waterleaf Family

OTHER NAME *Scorpion Weed*
HEIGHT *4″–20″/10–50 cm*
HABITAT *Dry hillsides, sandy soil, banks, alkaline flats; mountains*
SEASON *June–August in B.C.; May–July on prairies*

This delicately pretty flower is widespread in the dry interior of B.C., south-western Alberta, and south-eastern Saskatchewan; also in east and west Washington, western Oregon, and northern California. The genus comprises some 200 species, one of which (*P. franklinii*) has purplish flowers similar to but smaller than the one illustrated, and cut leaves instead of whole. It is found from Alberta to Manitoba. Some species are so minutely diverse as to defy many professional botanists; for instance there are about ten distinct leaf-types, from broad and pinnately cleft, through narrow and 'entire', to fern-like deeply cleft narrow leaves dissected like carrot leaves. The flowers may be light blue and pale violet or yellowish. One alpine species (*P. sericea*) is a beautiful violet-blue with silvery, silky leaves; it grows on screes and rockslides in Manning Park, B.C.

Phakelos—a fascicle or close bundle, is the Greek origin of the name, referring to the closely packed flowers at the head of the stem. *Linearis* means 'in a line' or 'linear', although this is not wholly descriptive, since the *phacelia* illustrated has three-lobed leaves as well as narrow ones.

Phlox diffusa Benth.

POLEMONIACEAE

SPREADING PHLOX Phlox Family

OTHER NAMES *None*
HEIGHT *2"–3"/5–7.5 cm*
HABITAT *Mountains*
SEASON *June–August*

Phlox is a Greek word meaning 'flame', referring to the bright colors (rather than to any shade of yellow) of this large and interesting group of plants. The one illustrated is an alpine plant with color variations from white through pink, pale lavender, purple, and even magenta, all within a few feet of one another. It is found in the mountains of B.C. and southwards on the west side of the Continental Divide to California. Many other species can be found in the prairie provinces and adjacent American states. The most similar to the one shown here has white flowers. Both grow in low, dense mats and create a carpet of blossom among the rocks.

Dwarf cultivated phloxes adorn many rock gardens. Wild ones are difficult to transplant, however, for they grow from a tap root that is difficult to dig intact; in any case these fragile blooms should be left for others to enjoy. Layering is a possible way of propagating without disturbing the plant, but of course you must know that you can return many months later when roots have been established.

Variations in the shape of the flowers occur frequently; some have flat, narrow petals and some, like the one illustrated, have rounded, slightly overlapping ones (the painting is enlarged—a life-size flower is shown below). If you open the corolla of a single blossom, you will find the stamens attached at different levels so that pollen from the anthers must fall on some part of an insect visitor's head as it searches for nectar (see inset). One of the diagnostic features of phlox species is the placement of the stamens inside the corolla, and the relative length of the style.

Phlox longifolia Nutt.

POLEMONIACEAE

LONG-LEAVED PHLOX Phlox Family

OTHER NAMES *None*
HEIGHT 8″–20″ / 20–50 cm
HABITAT *Dry plains, rocky places in mountains*
SEASON *June–July*

Like the spreading phlox (*P. diffusa*) on page 212, there are different colored members of this species to be seen growing within a few feet of each other, principally pink or white. Whereas dwarf phlox forms lovely cushions of pastel shades close to the ground, this one is much taller and has longer, thinner leaves arranged up the stem in pairs rather than whorls.

All phlox flowers are extremely delicate and will wither within a few minutes of picking. It is better to leave the plants to continue to carpet the hillsides.

The species illustrated is widespread in B.C. and the western United States in the East Cascade Mountains. Many very similar ones are to be seen in the prairie provinces and the plains states of the U.S.A.

Sisyrinchium douglasii Dietr.

IRIDACEAE

SATIN-FLOWER Iris Family

OTHER NAMES *Purple-eyed Grass, Grass-widows*
HEIGHT *6"–16"/15–40 cm*
HABITAT *Grassy woodlands, rock pockets; sea level to about
      6,000'/1,800 m*
SEASON *Mid-February – April*

Satin-flower's fragile, nodding blooms shimmer in pale sunlight and tremble with every breeze. It is probably the first flower of spring in western Canada. It grows in clumps of a dozen or more flower-stems, each bearing two flared blooms sheathed in papery bracts. This species grows in western B.C. and on Vancouver Island's southern tip, on both sides of the Cascade Mountains and south to California. Color variations occur in this as in so many flowers in a species; some may be pink, deep purple, or, rarely, white or striped. All have three brilliant orange anthers that are joined for about half their length; and each tepal (since sepals and petals are alike) has a tiny, characteristically pointed tip. (Inset: three petals removed to show joined filaments.)

Blue-eyed grass (*S. angustifolium*), whose flowers are pale blue or bluish purple, smaller and less spectacular than *S. douglasii*, grows from southern Alaska to Baja California, east across Canada and east of the Rocky Mountains in Montana and Wyoming.

The generic name is from an iris-like plant first named by the man who can be called the founder of botanical science: Theophrastus (c. 370–287 BC), a Greek philosopher who studied under Plato and Aristotle. He wrote a history of plants in ten volumes, one of the earliest works on botany to have come down to us. He also wrote eight books *On the Causes of Plants*, of which six are extant.

The specific name honors David Douglas, the English botanist who first described the plant when he found it just east of The Dalles on the Columbia River, in 1826.

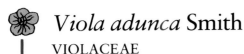

Viola adunca Smith

VIOLACEAE

WESTERN LONG-SPURRED VIOLET Violet Family

OTHER NAMES *Early Blue Violet, Hook Violet*
HEIGHT *2″–3″/5–7.5 cm*
HABITAT *Dry to moist meadows, woods, open ground, moist prairie,
        bluffs*
SEASON *April–June in B.C.; May–July on prairie*

Very shy women are sometimes described as 'shrinking violets', a romantic reference to the way the flower petals fold in. Sweet violets have been cultivated for centuries, several species being known to the early Romans; today some 900 species occur almost throughout the world. *Viola* (pronounced in the Latin manner with the accent on the first syllable) was the name given to those species known to the early Romans. The specific name *adunca* comes from *aduncus*, meaning hooked, referring to the spurred base of the lowest petal.

The violet illustrated here grows from B.C. to Manitoba with some fourteen other species, and it can be considered typical of the prairie provinces and adjacent American states. However, its range is so vast that it can be found throughout most of western North America and even eastwards to the Atlantic coast, where it blooms correspondingly later (approximately July–August).

While cross-pollination is ensured (notice the pencil bee guidelines leading to the pollen-covered anthers), violets do not rely on insects exclusively to propagate the species. When the flowers fade, curious cleistogamous (closed) flowers appear at or below ground level. Having no need for insects, they have dispensed with perfume or petals, and in fact the sepals never open. The enclosed stamens pollinate the pistil and the flower is thus self-fertilized. Viable seeds shoot outwards by explosion of the ripe capsules, to germinate several inches from the parent plant. The violet needs two strings to its bow: creatures, from deer to sparrows to slugs, feed on the flowers and a good crop must be produced to ensure that at least some plants survive to continue the race.

Viola palustris L.

VIOLACEAE

MARSH VIOLET Violet Family

OTHER NAME *Alpine Marsh Violet*
HEIGHT *2"–3" / 5–7.5 cm*
HABITAT *Peaty soil of swamps and wet meadows, wet borders of rivulets*
SEASON *May–June in B.C.; May–August elsewhere*

This violet is distinct from *V. adunca* (page 218) in several ways. Only the lowest petal is lined with purple and the flower color is more delicate; there are also white specimens with faint purple lines on the lower petal. The leaves are smooth, shiny, and firm, with the edges neatly scalloped (where the long-spurred violet has thinner, tooth-edged leaves with rounded or abruptly blunt tips). Furthermore, leaves and flowers grow directly from creeping rhizomes instead of branching above ground. The spur or nectary is much shorter than that of the long-spurred violet.

Marsh violet is found from B.C. to California, east to Manitoba, and more northerly to Labrador and Maine.

Distinguishing features of the many violet species are the various lengths of their nectaries—the spur behind the petals and the shapes of the leaves and the ways in which they grow—up the stems or directly from the ground. The marsh violet has a slender root with tufted stems rising from it.

Violets grow easily enough from seed but it is difficult to carry some of them successfully to maturity, let alone into bloom. You can try taking a small root section or a piece of root clump, being very careful to protect and moisten the extremely delicate root hairs. Of the four violet species portrayed in this book I have found *V. glabella* (page 88) the easiest to grow from seed. For some reason that I have yet to fathom, *V. adunca* (page 218) will not transplant even a couple of hundred feet to seemingly identical soil and aspect, and from many seedlings I still have but one blooming specimen.

BROWN TO GREEN

Asarum caudatum Lindl.

ARISTOLOCHIACEAE

WILD GINGER Birthwort Family

OTHER NAME *Ginger-root*
HEIGHT *Flower at ground level, leaves to 8"/20 cm*
HABITAT *Moist, rich soil, shady woods*
SEASON *May–June*

Because it flowers beneath its leaves, at ground level, and the blooms are brown, wild ginger is a difficult flower to find unless you recognize the heart-shaped, 'blistered' leaves, which rise in pairs above the single flower. The leaf-stems are irregularly covered with white hairs, which are very apparent when seen with the light behind them. The flower is of unusual shape and strange construction: petals are represented by tiny scales; the deeply cleft cup that looks like a flower is in fact made up of welded sepals divided into three lobes that extend into 2"/5 cm whip-like tails (Latin *cauda*—a tail) covered in fine red hairs. The stubby central pistil and twelve stamens are enclosed in a white square cunningly outlined in pointed arcs of purple (see inset of enlarged stamens, style, and ovary).

The flower changes color from glistening pinkish-brown in spring to a muddy purple-green after pollination by small flies, ants (which also disperse the seeds), or other creeping insects, and slugs. Butterflies and bees, apart from the fact that they do not frequent shady woods at ground level, cannot see the odd flower color. The edible rhizome has a ginger scent when crushed but the ginger of commerce is a tropical plant (*Zingiber* spp.). Indians, especially the Sechelt band on the west coast, crushed the leaves of *A. caudatum* for use as a poultice for cuts.

This is essentially a west-coast plant, which in certain locations on Vancouver Island may bloom from March into the summer. *A. canadense*, found in southern Manitoba and temperate zones in the eastern U.S.A., has the same coloring and shape but the sepals end in up-curving points instead of long tails.

Wild ginger transplants well from a piece of rhizome planted about an inch deep, with the leaf-tip above ground. After years in my wild garden it has not fulfilled its reputation of being an invasive weed.

Fritillaria lanceolata **Pursh**

LILIACEAE

CHOCOLATE LILY Lily Family

OTHER NAMES *Rice-root, Mission Bells*
HEIGHT *12"–18"/30–45 cm*
HABITAT *Grassy bluffs, moist banks, hedgerows; sea level to 5,000'/1,500 m*
SEASON *April–June*

You may easily miss this flower even while prowling carefully, but if you find it, notice the patterns of chocolate and green on the tepals, and the bright yellow anthers beneath them. There may be more than one flower to a stem in this species and another (*F. camschatcensis*) has several smaller, unmottled, purple-brown flowers to a stem, with leaves in whorls of five to ten at intervals up it.

The chocolate lily illustrated grows in south-western B.C. and in the south-eastern region of Vancouver Island, on both sides of the Cascade Mountains in Washington but on the west side in Oregon, south to California and in northern Idaho. *F. camschatcensis* is common on the B.C. coast, occasional in the inland Skeena and Bulkley Valleys.

Bulbs of the two species look alike, with many 'infants' attached to the parent (see inset); the whole growth is edible and was an important source of food for Indian peoples. The fact that the bulblets look like grains of cooked rice gives the plant one of its names, rice-root. *Fritillaria* comes from the Latin word *fritillus*—a dice-box, which in this case probably refers to the box-like shape of the seed capsule (see inset).

Harvest these lilies with a camera if you will—chocolate lily in particular makes a marvellous picture if you can find one with the sun behind it. Picking is likely to kill, since it removes leaves—the source of nourishment for the bulb beneath the soil.

Typha latifolia L.

TYPHACEAE

CATTAIL Cattail Family

OTHER NAMES *Cattail Flag, Broadleaf Cattail, Bulrush*
HEIGHT *4'–8'/12–24 dm*
HABITAT *Swamps, shallow lakeshores, wet ditches*
SEASON *August–November*

Cattail, or bulrush as it is also well known, is as versatile as it is familiar across southern Canada and much of the U.S.A. wherever there is shallow, standing, or slow-moving water. The pale brown terminal spike is the male or staminate flower-head consisting of hundreds of infinitesimal flowers spiralling round a central core. Below it is the sausage-shaped female head. The yellow blur in the illustration is pollen shed by the male. When seeds contained in the spongy tissue of the female flower are ripe, the whole structure explodes into millions of thread-like seed hairs, by which time the male flower has usually wilted and fallen, leaving the woody core.

Indians used the long slender leaves in house construction and to make mats. The incredibly fine 'down' (the seeds) served as insulation from cold and to stuff mattresses and pillows and light fires. Also, Blackfoot Indians made a pack of the down for the treatment of burns.

Young cattail flowers can be cooked like sweet corn and the roots can be eaten raw or cooked, as can the lower parts of the stems and leaves. New shoots taste like cucumber. Geese, muskrat, and elk love to feed on them and the plant creates valuable cover for many types of waterfowl and other birds. After pollen appears the flower-heads can be shaken into a bag; the pollen makes a tasty and colorful addition to flour used for making breads or cakes: they turn out a beautiful yellow. Flower-heads may be cut for house decoration without damaging the plant because it also reproduces from creeping underwater rhizomes.

Typha latifolia was known to the ancient Greeks as *typhe*. The name 'bulrush' is wrongly applied to this genus owing to the error made by Victorian painters who depicted Moses among the 'bulrushes' (*T. latifolia*). They were not aware that the biblical plant was the Egyptian bulrush or papyrus (*Cyperus papyrus* L.), which has smooth, three-sided stems 8'–16'/2–5 m tall, topped by a mop-like panicle of small florets like grass. This is the bulrush quoted in Exodus 2:3—'she took for him an ark of bulrushes'; and in Isaiah 18:2—'in vessels of bulrushes upon the waters. . . .'

This extremely versatile bulrush was made into paper by Egyptians, Greeks, and Romans, and until the twelfth century by later Italians; young shoots were eaten locally; stems served as fuel in an almost fuelless land; the stout rootstocks tasted sweet like licorice. Modern Abyssinians still

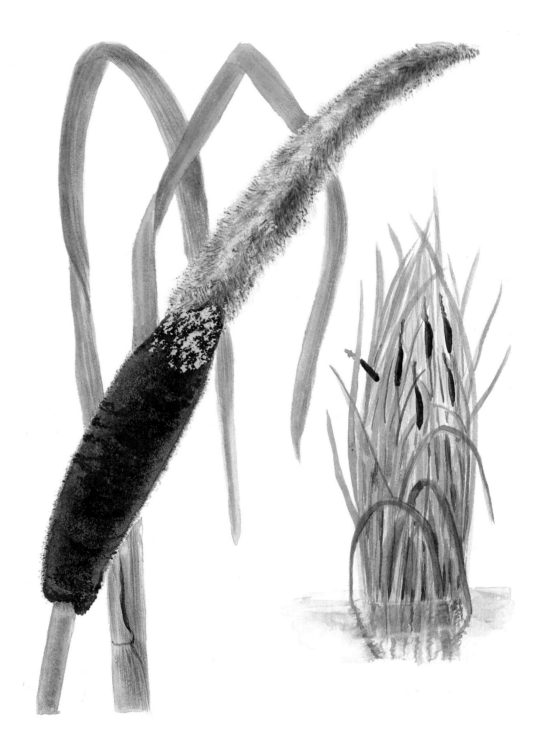

make small boats from it—shades of Kon-Tiki!

Today the name bulrush is used for a genus (*Scirpus*) of marsh plants that bear round, spiky leaves rising stiffly from the water in dark green clumps. At least one species (*S. acutus*) is used for making mats and chair-seats. The derivation of the common name is Middle English *bule*—bull (in this sense 'large') and *rish*—rush.

Thalictrum occidentale Gray

RANUNCULACEAE

MEADOW RUE Buttercup Family

OTHER NAMES *Maid-of-the-Mist, Western Meadow Rue*
HEIGHT *18"–24"/45–60 cm*
HABITAT *Open woodland spaces or beneath deciduous trees;
            streambanks*
SEASON *May–August*

This is one of the most delicate and unusual flowers of damp woods. On a sunless day the plant may pass unnoticed, the lacy blue-green leaves and small green or purple flowers blending inconspicuously with the other greens of the forest floor. The leaves are so thin that they hardly seem to have three dimensions.

Male and female flowers are borne on different plants (dioecious) to avoid self-fertilization (see inset), and each may be a considerable distance from the other. Since the male flower has no petals, only green sepals and purple stamens, and since the female is a dull purple—a color not seen well by bees—one wonders how the species propagates. In fact, flying insects that inhabit shady woods are attracted to the male by a gland at the base of the sepals that emits a perfume too subtle for 'the noselessness of man'. The multitude of minute pollen grains is also wind-dispersed; this gives the plant two chances, even if the second is somewhat more haphazard than the first.

Meadow rue species are found in all the western provinces—the one illustrated from B.C. to Saskatchewan and south to north-east California; Manitoba has a relative almost exactly like it.

The generic name has its root in the Greek word *thal*—producing young shoots; *occidentale* means 'of the west' (western hemisphere). Rue (*Ruta graveolens*) is the Old World herb that first appeared in 1382 in Wycliffe's Bible—'Woe to you, Pharisees, that tythe mint and rue' (Luke 11:42). The plants of this genus have long been known to have bitter medicinal properties in their roots and leaves. And one must not forget Ophelia's flower—'You must wear your rue with a difference.'

Glossary

corolla (petals)

calyx (sepals)

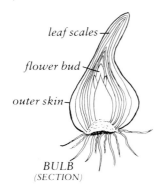

leaf scales

flower bud

outer skin

BULB
(SECTION)

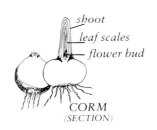

shoot

leaf scales

flower bud

CORM
(SECTION)

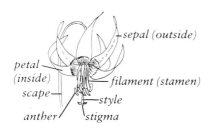

sepal (outside)

petal
(inside)

scape

anther

filament (stamen)

style

stigma

LILY

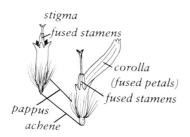

stigma

fused stamens

corolla
(fused petals)

fused stamens

pappus

achene

COMPOSITE

ACHENE A small, hard, dry one-seeded fruit that does not open when ripe.
ANTHER Pollen-bearing tip of the (male) stamen.
AXIL The upper angle formed where a leaf-stalk joins a stem.

BRACT A modified leaf, usually small, from the axil of which a flower may arise.
BULB A swollen underground shoot consisting of a very short stem covered with thick, fleshy leaves that serve a storage function; roots are produced from the base. May live indefinitely as a single unit or increase by splitting (e.g. onion, daffodil).

CALYX All the sepals of a flower, collectively.
CILIATE Having a marginal fringe of hairs.
CLEISTOGAMOUS A flower that sets seeds without opening.
COLUMN Organ formed by the union of stamens and pistils in orchids.
CORM An enlarged underground stem covered with thin scale-like leaves, externally like a bulb but internally solid. Matures and dies after one year's growth, being replaced by a new corm or corms on top, beside or beneath the old one (e.g. crocus).
COROLLA Flower petals collectively, whether fused or separate.

DIOECIOUS Male and female flowers on separate plants.
DISK In orchids, the face or upper surface of the lip; also refers to the central part of the head of members of the Composite Family.
DISK FLOWER Small tubular flowers in the center of a composite inflorescence (e.g. tiny yellow flowers in the center of a sunflower).

FILAMENT The stalk of a stamen.
FLORET Small flower; individual flower in a cluster in the Composite Family.

INFLORESCENCE Arrangement of flowers in a cluster or head.
INVOLUCRE A whorl of bracts beneath a flower or flower cluster.

KEEL A sharply defined longitudinal ridge; also two partly fused lower petals of many Pea Family flowers.

LIP The odd petal of an orchid; also one of the divisions of a two-lipped corolla or calyx.

MENTUM Spur-like projection formed by sepals and extended foot of the column in an orchid.

NECTARY Any structure that produces and contains nectar (e.g. the spur of a violet; columbine).
NODE Place on a stem that bears a leaf or whorl of leaves from which roots may arise in some species.

OVARY The expanded basal part of a pistil that contains ovules.
OVULE Immature seed.

PAPPUS The modified calyx limb—hairs, awns, or scales at the base of the corolla or the tip of the achene in the Composite Family.
PARASITE Growing on and deriving nourishment from another living plant.
PEDICEL The stalk of a single flower in a flower cluster.

233

Entire Leaf

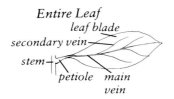

Entire Leaf

leaf blade
secondary vein
stem
petiole   main vein

disk floret
ray floret
bract
receptacle

leaf

RHIZOME

root
hair roots

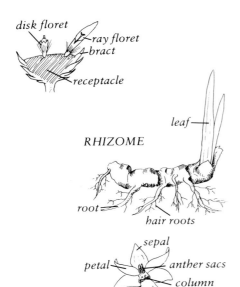

sepal
petal
anther sacs
column
ovary
lip
bract
spur

ORCHID

sessile leaf (no petiole)

leaflets
compound leaf
stipules

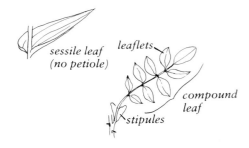

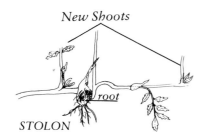

New Shoots

root

STOLON

PEDUNCLE The stalk of a flower-cluster or of a single flower.

PETALOID Sepals that look like petals (e.g. yellow water lily).

PETIOLE A leaf-stalk.

PINNATE Feather-like; compound leaf with leaflets arranged on each side of petiole.

PISTIL Female organ of a flower; comprises stigma, style, and ovary.

PLACENTA Structure inside the ovary to which ovules are attached, from which they are released at maturity (e.g. milkweed).

POD Dry fruit that splits open to release seed (e.g. fireweed).

PUBESCENT Having hairs, usually soft or downy.

RACEME An elongated flower cluster along a single stalk with each flower having a pedicel, the youngest at the top.

RAY FLOWER Flower that looks like a petal; the outer ring of flattened, elongated 'petals' in the heads of many composites.

RECEPTACLE The upper end of the pedicel (stalk) to which flower parts are attached; in the Composite Family, the end of the peduncle to which the flowers of the head are attached.

RENIFORM Kidney-shaped.

RHIZOME An elongated, horizontal, creeping underground stem (e.g. iris).

SAC A sac or pouch (e.g. lady's slipper).

SAPROPHYTE A plant that lives on dead organic matter, neither parasitical nor able to make its own food.

SCAPE A stem rising from the ground, naked or without ordinary foliage.

SEPAL One of the outermost set of floral leaves, usually green or greenish, leaf-like in shape and texture.

SESSILE Without a stalk.

SPADIX A dense or fleshy spike of flowers (e.g. skunk cabbage).

SPATHE A large, generally solitary bract, often colored, below and usually enclosing a spadix or other inflorescence (e.g. skunk cabbage).

SPIKE An elongated flower cluster like a raceme (see above) with stalkless or nearly stalkless flowers (e.g. rattlesnake plaintain).

SPUR A hollow pocket, part of a corolla or calyx (e.g. violet).

STAMEN Male organ of a flower; a filament topped by an anther carrying pollen.

STANDARD The uppermost or 'flying' petal of a flower in the Pea Family.

STIGMA The part of the pistil (female organ) receptive to pollen.

STIPULE One of a pair of basal appendages found on many leaves.

STOLON An elongated, horizontal, surface-creeping stem capable of reproducing at its nodes (e.g. wild strawberry).

STYLE Slender stalk connecting the stigma to the ovary in the pistil.

TEPAL Sepals and petals that look alike in form and color (e.g. calypso).

UMBEL Flower cluster with all the pedicels arising from the same point (e.g. cow parsnip).

UTRICLE Small thin-walled, one-seeded, more or less inflated fruit.

WHORL A ring of three or more similar organs (e.g. leaves) radiating from a common point (e.g. tiger lily).

WING One of the two lateral petals in a flower in the Pea Family; any thin, flat projection or extension.

Selected References

BARBER, Lynn, *Heyday of Natural History 1820–1870*, 1980, Jonathan Cape Ltd., London.

BREITUNG, A.J., *A Botanical Survey of the Cypress Hills*, 1954, Can. Field Naturalist, Vol. 68, #2, 55–92.

BUDD, A.C., & BEST, K.F., *Wild Plants of the Canadian Prairies*, 1969, Canada Dept. of Agriculture, Ottawa.

CLARK, L.J., *Wild Flowers of British Columbia*, 1973, Gray's Publishing Ltd., Sidney, B.C.

CORMACK, R.G.H., *Wild Flowers of Alberta*, 1967, Gov't of Alberta, Edmonton.

CRAIGHEAD, J.J., & CRAIGHEAD, F.C., Jr., *A Field Guide to Rocky Mountain Wildflowers From Northern Arizona and New Mexico to British Columbia*, 1963, Houghton Mifflin Company, Boston, Mass.

DAVIES, John, *Douglas of the Forests*, 1980, Univ. of Washington Press, Seattle.

DOUGLAS, Geo. W., *The Sunflower Family (Asteraceae) of British Columbia, Vol. 1— Senecioneae*, 1982, Occasional Papers Series #23, British Columbia Provincial Museum, Victoria, B.C.

FRASER, W.P., & RUSSELL, R.C., *An Annotated List of the Plants of Saskatchewan*, 1954, Univ. of Saskatchewan, Saskatoon.

HASKIN, L.L., *Wild Flowers of the Pacific Coast*, 1934, Binfords & Mort, Portland, Ore.

HENSHAW, Julia W., *Wild Flowers of the North American Mountains*, 1917, Rob't McBride & Co., New York.

HITCHCOCK, C.L., & CRONQUIST, A., *Flora of the Pacific Northwest*, 1973, Univ. of Washington Press, Seattle and London.

HITCHCOCK et al., *Vascular Plants of the Pacific Northwest*, 5 vols., 1955–69, Univ. of Washington Press, Seattle and London.

KOZLOFF, Eugene N., *Plants and Animals of the Pacific Northwest*, 1976, Univ. of Washington Press, Seattle.

LINNAEUS, Carl, *Species Plantarum; 1753, Vols. I–II*, Facsimile First Edn., introduction by W.T. Stearn, 1954, The Ray Society, London.

LYONS, C.P., *Trees, Shrubs and Flowers to Know in British Columbia*, 1954, J.M. Dent & Sons (Canada) Ltd. and The Wrigley Printing Co. Ltd., Vancouver, B.C.

MEEUSE, B.J.D., *The Story of Pollination*, 1961, Ronald Press Co., New York.

MOLDENKE, H.N. & A.L., *Plants of the Bible*, 1952, Ronald Press Co., New York.

MONTGOMERY, F.H., *Plants From Sea to Sea*, 1966, The Ryerson Press, Toronto.

MOSS, E.H., *Flora of Alberta*, 1959, Univ. of Toronto Press, Toronto.

RYDBERG, P.A., *Flora of the Prairies & Plains of Central North America*, 1932, The New York Botanical Garden, New York.

SCOGGAN, H.J., *Flora of Manitoba Bulletin #140*, 1957, National Museum of Canada, Dept. of Northern Affairs & National Resources, Ottawa.

SZCZAWINSKI, A.F., *The Heather Family of British Columbia, #19*, 1962, British Columbia Provincial Museum, Victoria, B.C.

_____ & HARDY, G.A., *Guide to Common Edible Plants of British Columbia, #20*, 1962, British Columbia Provincial Museum, Victoria, B.C.

_____ *The Orchids of British Columbia, #16*, 1970, British Columbia Provincial Museum, Victoria, B.C.

TAYLOR, T.M.C., *The Pea Family of British Columbia*, #32, 1974, British Columbia
    Provincial Museum, Victoria, B.C.
_____ *The Figwort Family of British Columbia*, #33, 1974, British Columbia Provincial
    Museum, Victoria, B.C.
_____ *The Lily Family of British Columbia, #25*, 1966, British Columbia Provincial
    Museum, Victoria, B.C.
_____ *The Rose Family of British Columbia, #30*, 1973, British Columbia Provincial
    Museum, Victoria, B.C.

VANCE, F.R. et al., *Wildflowers Across the Prairies*, 1977, Western Producer Prairie Books,
    Saskatoon, Sask.

Index

The usual method of indexing families in groups is not practical in a book based on color grouping. For readers who wish to make comparisons between one member of a family and others, English and Latin family names are printed in CAPITALS, followed by page numbers where members of each family will be found.

Common names are printed in Roman type. Scientific names are printed in *italics*.

options:

    under broad-leaf cattail

    -leaved marigold 4

for dog-toothed violet

    -tooth violet 58

(options from previous settings) for
  Habenaria

    leucostachys 28

    Leucostachys 29